HOW TO STAY AFLOAT WEARING ARMY BOOTS

William T. Melms

EAGLE EDITIONS
2004

EAGLE EDITIONS
AN IMPRINT OF HERITAGE BOOKS, INC.

Books, CDs, and more—Worldwide

For our listing of thousands of titles see our website
at
www.HeritageBooks.com

Published 2004 by
HERITAGE BOOKS, INC.
Publishing Division
65 East Main Street
Westminster, Maryland 21157-5026

COPYRIGHT © 2004 WILLIAM T. MELMS

All rights reserved. No part of this book may be reproduced or transmitted in any form or by any means, electronic or mechanical, including photocopying, recording or by any information storage and retrieval system without written permission from the author, except for the inclusion of brief quotations in a review.

International Standard Book Number: 0-7884-2532-3

To Jack LaZebnik

He who taught me that there is no sin in syntactics

Thanks for listening,
Bill Melmer

ACKNOWLEDGEMENTS

It was Robert and Jack LaZebnik who convinced me that misadventure can be as appealing to the reader as well-intentioned heroics. It was Bob, the larger of the two, who strong-armed me into putting on paper those courageous mistakes that kept us afloat, but lost most of the time.

Thanks to the blond bomb shell, Maryann Talbot, for her word processing and enforcement of deadlines.

To Nancy Rosenfeld, agent, for encouragement and cultured drum beating.

Appreciation to the Army Transportation Museum at Fort Eustise, Virginia for helping me spell correctly the names of those unpronounceable exotic places.

Special thanks to my most tolerant editor, Jack LaZebnik, who stayed the course whatever the weather.

With help like this, who needs an author?

How to Stay Afloat Wearing Army Boots

Chapter One

It seems appropriate at this time, after the recent commemoration of D-Day and the invasion of Europe, that we remember the UNSUNG heroes of World War II. Now I may not have been a recorded hero, but I was certainly UNSUNG. I was not even allowed to hum the National Anthem. According to the Department of Defense (DOD to you military types) my voice would give Aid and Comfort to the enemy. This may be a long narrative because it was a long war. Mother always said that if I had fought as hard in the Army as I did to stay out of it, the war would have ended sooner. Last December 7th the local radio station called to ask what my reaction was in 1941 when I heard about the bombing of Pearl Harbor. "I remembered in vivid detail…damn it, there goes my deferment!"

I do sort of have military background that allows me to speak with some authority. My great Uncle Elmo served in the Spanish War. He tried to dodge the draft by acquiring a wife. He tricked my aunt into marrying him. He told her she was pregnant. Uncle Elmo always insisted the really big one was the war with Spain. Until the day he gave his final salute while reciting the Pledge of Allegiance, he claimed World War One was a press agents trick to sell war bonds. He refought his war every night at the dinner table and concluded his lecture with "no one would dare to start a war today after what Teddy Roosevelt and I did to the Spanish at San Juan Hill." Actually, Uncle Elmo never got on that boat to Cuba. He picked up a case of mumps and spent the next seven months serving honorably fitting shoes to recruits at the Fort Meyers army depot.

When my "neighbors and friends," affectionately known as the Draft Board, honored me by providing the opportunity to defend my country, Uncle Elmo said, "Don't worry son, it will be like a country club compared to Camp Pickett. They don't have wars like they used to. Everybody's too soft." Today, I'm beginning to feel a little like Uncle Elmo. I can remember when the expression "a car with four on the floor" meant a double date at a drive in movie, and "safe sex" was a weekend when your parents were out of town.

The possibility that there was a military career in my future was brought to my attention with the announcement of a Peace Time Army being formed to provide the youth of America with a year of healthful recreation under the direction of Uncle Sam and a kindly first sergeant who would serve as a surrogate father, guiding my every move while I savored America's great outdoors and mess hall food. All expenses paid (except laundry), plus twenty-one dollars a month. Of course, no one in his right mind volunteered for this opportunity so patriotism was encouraged with a little help from neighbors and friends through a support group known as Selective Service.

The popular game of the period was *Beat the Draft*, or *How to Fake It*. The first obstacle to overcome was the draft board doctor. To qualify as a draft board examining physician, the doctor had to have a mean streak. Prescribed decor for the examining room included a plaque which read "Fight For Your Country or Go Back Where You Came From." At this point, in my case, it seemed that "join 'em approach" would be the most prudent action to take. I bounded into his office and announced, "Doc, I'm sure glad they finally got to me!" The good doctor's stethoscope nearly fell off his ears. When He recovered he squinted and asked, why? I dodged the obvious answers but reluctantly broke down and confessed that I was faking good health just to get into the Army and get some free much needed medical attention. Now, there is nothing that can turn a well-trained doctor into a pathetic trauma victim quicker than the words "free medical service" unless it's socialized medicine. I told him about these occasional, but unimportant fainting spells which, I was certain, skilled Army doctors could clear up in no time. After a few moments of soul-searching, he finally said "Go home and let me review the matter." I knew victory was in my grasp. He was a well-trained physician and there could be only one answer—4F, unfit for military duty, a potential draftee's dream! A badge to wear proudly. I had outsmarted the system.

Then, like the rest of the world, I was double-crossed—Pearl Harbor. Once again I was called before my friendly doctor, who was now smiling. As I walked through the door, he handed me my 1-A fit-for-service card. "Doc" I said, "don't you want me to take my clothes off and cough? And what about my fainting spells?" His response was, "You don't even have to take your hat off. And we've determined the cause of your fainting; you're allergic to those cheap polyester suits you've been wearing. We're going to put you in pure wool and sensible shoes. The only thing you'll have to worry about is occasionally somebody trying to shoot you." Of course I appealed this unfair decision and appeared before the board which was headed by an easygoing lady who reminds me now of Leona Helmsy. I asked her what the alternative was and she said something like three years in jail.

We've all heard about recruits being shipped directly to war zones without training or preparation. Scary places like North Korea, Vietnam, Anzio, Normandy Beachhead. In my case it was worse. I was sent directly to Fort Custer at Battle

Creek. Now I understand the reason for Fort Custer. Ten days there and you're ready to volunteer for a Kamikaze mission just to leave. About the lowest person on the world totem pole is a recruit at an Army reception center. At that point you know there are two and a half million people authorized to give you orders. However, if you should be given KP duty that figure jumps to over three million because now all the buck privates can kick you around. I enjoyed KP for four straight 14-hour days and then was promoted to the garbage truck. The drivers insisted that I ride sitting on top of our odious cargo because my presence in the cab offended their olfactory organs. It was not the best of times.

Finally I reached the apex of my Custer experience. The psychological examination to keep square pegs from ending up in round holes--where with the misstroke of a pen I was classified as a qualified Maritime Second Mate. Although at the time I didn't know the bow from the stern, today I do know that the pointy end is the bow.

It was comforting to learn that a qualified psychiatrist would interview me at the reception center and make certain that my inherent skills and modestly enviable intellect would be recognized and utilized to the Army's best advantage. It was disappointing to discover that my buck-private examiner had been inducted the day before and because the KP roster was filled for that period had been assigned to the recruit processing division as a "psychological examiner." One way of keeping idle hands busy. In civilian life he had been a butter-packer with a reading deficiency making it difficult to convey adequately to me the pre-printed questions intended to uncover some hidden talent that, if properly utilized, would bring the war to an early close. It became increasingly embarrassing to realize what little talent I had for leading our troops out of the trenches. Newspaper reporter, advertising salesman, freelance bartender--nothing we were fighting to preserve. I became convinced it was better to know the questions than the answers.

Finally, we reached the section on Hobbies. The only activity I could recall, other than drive-in movies and six-pack bowling binges, was the half ownership of a leaky 16-foot sailboat that could never make it across Lake St. Claire. It was close to chow time and my interrogator was getting hungry; with a cry of victory he noted my use of the word "boat" and the printed classification of "Maritime-Second Mate" on the Army qualification form. With a flourish of his government issue pen, he X'd in the box that instantly provided me with a past, present, and military future. It was a heady moment for both of us. The interview was over. We headed for the mess hall together, although already I did feel a little superior; now I was a soldier with a profession and a mission.

Chapter Two

Life didn't seem to improve. There was no insignia to distinguish me from the rank and file. I was still taking orders, learning how to make up a bunk so firmly that a quarter would bounce smartly off the blanket, scrubbing a barracks floor to the point of turning the boards to pulp wood, and saluting everything that moved. Never did learn how to fire a rifle--apparently future admirals would not be required to shoulder arms.

Finally, orders came transferring me to a "Boat" company near Seattle, thirty-five miles from the closest water. The confused company commander must have fouled up somewhere in his past for now he was to use his infantry experience to turn us into first rate sailors. He knew his objective but wondered how he would reach it when the only water in the area was in Lister bags. The outline of the ship was scratched out on the parade ground and we practiced tying knots until some of is got so good we had to be cut out of our shoelaces at night.

Then it happened. Some one in the Pentagon must have seen my personnel file and wondered what a "qualified Maritime Officer" was doing as an enlisted man, risking his life on an unseaworthy vessel in the middle of a parade ground. Orders came through immediately discharging me as an EM and commissioning me a second lieutenant. A rapid and well-deserved rise from kitchen police to officer class in three months, without basic training. It was a conundrum to my company commander as well. What would he do with a newly made shave-tail who could no longer train with the unit because, according to the Department of Defense, he was already a fully-trained qualified Maritime Officer?

To solve the problem, orders were cut placing me on temporary day duty aboard a two-hundred ten foot marine salvage vessel doing daily shakedown cruises on Puget Sound. The Cheakamus was seventy-two-year old coal burning steamer the Canadian government had abandoned as unfit for sea duty.

Turning this venerable craft over to the United States was like recycling old clothes at a Goodwill store. Capably commanding the Cheakamus was salty old Colonel Jacobs, an experienced World War I Navy retread. Not wanting to stay at home to wash windows for his wife, Colonel Jacobs volunteered to take over this part of the Army's navy. For three weeks the ship returned to the pier each night, thankful it was still afloat. It was expected that after each day of cruising I would be trucked back to camp in time for evening chow. Something must have been lost in the translation. Unknown to me, the day I reported aboard for my temporary training was the day the Cheakamus was setting sail for the Aleutian Islands. I was being Shanghaied and didn't know it! I suspect it was a plot by my CO at the parade ground to move me on to greater things and out of his troubled table of organization.

Shortly after casting off, I was leaning on the rail with a fellow officer and asked what time he expected us to be back at the pier in Seattle. Instead of checking his watch, he pulled out a pocket calendar and said, "Around the end of February." I shrieked, "That's four months from now! I'm due back at camp by 1700 hours—I'll be AWOL!" In a nonchalant manner he explained that we were on our way back to Dutch

Harbor in the Aleutians where the wind never stops blowing and the sun never shines. He also pointed out that I had been assigned as second mate and my watch began on the bridge at 2000 hours. I asked him where the bridge was. He liked my sense of humor.

In desperation, I rushed to find the Colonel and explained that I was not part of his crew, but that I had belonged to the 342 Boat Company with the dusty but safe parade ground, and that I must be back before taps. He was a burly man who seemed to have more important matters to handle, such as keeping the bilge pumps running. He said that if I was really determined to get back I might consider swimming. However, he did radio headquarters to inform them of the situation. Later, with the look of disappointment, he informed me there was no longer a problem. Army personnel people had solved it neatly by cutting new orders transferring me from the 342nd to the Cheakamus as Second Mate.

"Now, you belong to me," the Colonel said sadly.

It was dark and cold when I finally found the bridge and reported for my watch. It seemed lonesome up there. A kid stood at the wheel and the officer of the watch was drinking coffee in the chart room. When he saw me he snapped to attention and said, "Am I relieved?" I told him I was pleased that he was relieved, and because of that I was relieved, too. He looked at me kind of funny and pointed to some chicken scratches on a chart and asked whether I would accept it as our position. Of course I did. If it was good enough for him, it was good enough for me. At last I was alone and in command. It was lonesome and scary with nothing to see but a wall of blackness we seemed to be cutting through. The wheelsman asked if I wished to change course. I asked if he was happy with the present one. He just shrugged, so I told him to stick with it. My first command! Later in the watch I moved to the open wing of the bridge and peered into the cold darkness and wondered where I would be right now if that kid at Fort Custer had classified me as a brain surgeon. Suddenly at my side I detected the bulky bundled-up figure of the Colonel. It seemed he had difficulty sleeping, thinking about me guiding his ship through the Juan deFuca Straits. Our conversation was friendly but his questions seemed to be leading to a conclusion I was trying to avoid. Eventually he asked the size of the largest ship I had ever been on. After some backing and filling (that's a Navy expression) I mentioned the sixteen-foot sailboat that had succumbed to dry rot when we forgot to provide ventilation during storage. The Colonel was not pleased and exploded with, "My God! What farmer have they sent me now for a second mate?" He was wrong of course; I had never been on a farm. After cooling off, he explained that we would be gone four months and unless I had learned to be a sailor by the time we returned he would personally make me wish I had been "born a girl baby." This was not an encouraging way to start a nautical career.

It is customary aboard ship that the second mate also serves as navigating officer. This was a problem for someone having some difficulty trying to discern such nautical terms as port and starboard. I did know that port was a soothing after dinner wine and that (I assumed) starboard might be a tuna appetizer. The Colonel did his best to teach me the difference between hard right and full astern, but after I slid the Cheakamus onto a mud bank entering Ketchikan Harbor (I couldn't remember whether it was "red light returning" or "always add easterly deviation when correcting") he changed my secondary classification to "morale officer."

I will spare the reader details of my many learning experiences that occurred during that unplanned voyage to the Aleutians only because relating them might bring comfort to our nation's potential enemies. The culminating point of the Colonel's confidence in me became apparent when we reached Dutch Harbor. It was mid-afternoon when we dropped anchor with a dozen other ships to await orders. The Colonel told me I had anchor watch and he turned in for a nap. I wasn't sure what anchor watch meant, but I assumed it was that someone might steal the anchors. Seemed silly; here on the edge of the Arctic Circle there wasn't a scrap metals dealer within a thousand miles. Confident that the hooks were safe, I found an old deck chair in which I reclined and watched the clouds swinging around in complete circles, a phenomenon I attributed to high latitude--a theory I discovered later that was not inclusively correct. Suddenly in the middle of my celestial contemplation, frantic blinker messages from shore stations told us an enemy air attack was on the way. All ships in the harbor were to disperse immediately! Here was an action. Finally, a chance to see war close up. The Colonel raced to the bridge, seized the bullhorn and in stentorian voice ordered me to raise the anchors, now!

I saluted smartly, pleased with his trust, turned on the two windlasses and stood by as the anchors began to come up. Then something went wrong.

The chains came up about four feet and then, with an alarming clang, stopped. The relief valves on the windlasses popped and spouted steam across the foredeck. The Colonel on the bridge began to shriek in a most unofficer-like manner, demanding to know what was happening. I peered over the side and was horrified to note that the chains were neatly braided together and jammed in the hause holes. Now I knew what anchor watch meant, and why those clouds had been going around and around. It was really the ship. By this time we were the only vessel left in the harbor, and I often wonder what that lone Japanese pilot thought when he saw that single ship going around in circles trying to unbraid its anchor chains. When the matter was finally cleared and we were ready to move out, the all clear sounded and the other ships returned to anchorage.

The Colonel was not pleased. Actually he was livid and embarrassed by the ribbing from the other skippers who had witnessed the snafu in the afternoon. I tried to point out what a valuable "hands on" learning experience this had been for me. He muttered something about putting hands on me.

When we returned to Seattle it was time, after several other learning experiences, for Colonel Jacobs to make out my quarterly evaluation and fitness report. In the military, there are four ratings: Superior, Excellent, Good, and Unsatisfactory. To receive "Unsatisfactory" is tantamount to utter disgrace and the officer is usually discharged from the service. In wartime he might be reassigned as a mess hall commander in lower Slobvia. *Superior* is unheard of and is usually reserved for relatives of the President or to sons of heavy contributors to the party in power. *Excellent* really means *Satisfactory* and is the rating almost everyone gets. *Good* means the officer is really unsatisfactory, but who has the heart to ruin someone's military career?

In my case, the Colonel called upon his years of military experience to make the right decision--for him. He said that if he gave me the unsatisfactory rating there was the chance that he would be stuck with me for the rest of the war. But if he had rated me Superior, some self-serving S.O.B. who out-ranked him would steal me away from him.

He was so right. Three weeks after receiving my Superior rating, I was transferred to New Orleans, promoted to Captain, and given a ship of my own! What a feeling—nine-hundred thirty-five tons of steel, twin diesels turning with enough HP to move the Queen Mary, and the opportunity for a new learning experience! I was pleased with my crew of sixteen until I learned two of them had SUPERIOR ratings.

How to Stay Afloat Wearing Army Boots

Chapter Three

Anchors, with their intimidating size and weight, seemed determined to undermine my career as a Marine officer. The FS344 had been anchored in the middle of the Mississippi for three weeks before becoming my responsibility. Each day, the eight mph current dug the flukes a little deeper into the muddy river bottom. My first command to my new crew was to raise the anchors—after making certain the chains were free and unencumbered; there would be no repeat of the Aleutian incident. After a couple of initial tugs, the hooks began coming up smartly. But, just as they reach the hause holes, the kid on the bow announced—no anchor at the end of the starboard chain. I had buried an eighteen-hundred dollar United States Army anchor forever in the silt and mud at the bottom of the Mississippi River. The owner's manual did not tell me that to raise an embedded anchor you move the ship forward to shorten the chain and that tilts the anchor until the flukes are free to break out of the mud. Another learning experience. The Army began threatening to take the eighteen-hundred dollars out of my pay. Fortunately, and with some creative writing, we were able to "document" that a severe hurricane in the area had precipitated the conditions that led to the unavoidable loss of an anchor.

It was "Snuffy" our oldest enlisted crewman, who clued me in on how to beat the rap. Snuffy had been in the Army for seventeen years and had never risen higher that PFC. When we got him, he had just been busted back to buck private. He was a "guard house lawyer," gifted enough to keep everyone but himself out of trouble. Prior to the war, Snuffy had deserted from the peacetime army and thought he had beaten the system. Actually, the authorities knew where he was, but didn't want to take the time and trouble to pick him up. The military was getting along just fine without him. Then came Pearl Harbor and Snuffy was snatched back into service, given the choice of "volunteering" for the duration or spending five years in a jail cell. When he found out the Post Exchange sold his precious snuff at half the price he was paying at Rexall, active service was his choice.

Snuffy was a lousy seaman, but his latrine legal advice was invaluable. I made certain he stayed close to me as a sort of unofficial adjutant general. Whenever some bureaucratic paper shuffler ashore would charge me with "unauthorized procedures" or disregard of some vague Civil War regulation, Snuffy provided me with an excuse that looked great on paper and it was always accepted at headquarters because they couldn't figure out what he was talking about. Snuffy always said the military, like the IRS, loves documents, and if you made your plea on the right sized paper, in the proper form and with the required number of copies, you would invariably be exonerated from any charges short of treason. The formula seemed to work, but not for Snuffy. He was his own worst client. Much later on, when the ship was holed up in Tarpon Springs while a hurricane raged in the Gulf, he married the mayor's daughter. The Mayor of Tarpon Springs and his family, in addition to the Mayor's official duties, did our laundry for us. Much superior than the Quartermaster service on an Army base where our shirts came back with a permanent waffle-iron pattern. The Mayor's price was right, too. He accepted government issue canned food in lieu of cash. Our mistake was to use Snuffy to deliver and pick up the laundry. As soon as he saw the Mayor's daughter, he was in love. He proposed to her on the spot, and when he came for the finished laundry the next day she accepted. The Mayor was also an ordained minister and proudly performed the ceremony that united the happy couple. We didn't have crossed swords for them to walk under, but we did find a supply of boat hooks in the hold which served as well.

There was just one problem. Snuffy already had a wife in Atlanta and another in Boise, Idaho. Some one must have tipped off the Mayor. The day after the wedding, he contacted the personnel division at the Pentagon and learned that although he may have lost a daughter he had gained two daughter-in-laws, twice removed. Pentagon records were not completely accurate; they didn't know about the wife in Boise. The honeymoon was a short one. Something like five hours until a jeep pulled on to the pier and charged Snuffy with bigamy and hauled him away. It was a sad parting for me. Now I had to create my own cover stories for those minor inventory discrepancies—like the missing twenty-four government bed sheets the newlywed couple had taken.

The hurricane alert was lifted the next day and we headed for the Canal Zone. Snuffy had trained me well. I did send forth, out of heartfelt gratitude, a recommendation that he be promoted to corporal, although stockade commanders adhered to some preposterous regulation that inmates in their charge were not eligible for promotion and that my request would be filed in my own 201 file endorsed with a question mark.

My first voyage in command of the FS344, from New Orleans to the Gulf, was uneventful. With the river current propelling us in the right direction and riverbanks within sight on both sides, there was no chance of getting lost. My signal man (we called him "Sparks" like they did in John Wayne

Navy films) had just graduated from the Army Signal School at Fort Monmouth, New Jersey, and proudly carried a certificate attesting to his proficiency in Semaphore—but no mention of blinker training. Since the Civil War, the Army does not accept or believe there is any form of field communication other than the Semaphore. Boy Scouts are noted for the merit badges they earn for waving flags. No one has ever explained to the Army's Navy that under radio blackout in wartime ships talk to each other with blinker signals; hence, we had signalmen on other crafts who thought we were celebrating Bastille Day at sea. The FS344 was equipped with a state of the art blinker lamp, mounted on a three-hundred sixty degree swivel base. Our Sparks thought it was a family size barbecue grill.

When we reached the mouth of the Mississippi at the South Pass sea buoy about dusk, a far-off Navy shore station began sending furious blinker signals to us. Of course our signalman couldn't read them and finally decided the Navy signaler wanted to practice with him. He had deciphered the word "practice." I thought it was a wonderful idea and that our Sparks might learn to read blinker through friendly conversation with his Navy counterpart.

We sailed into the Gulf completely blacked out to avoid detection by any lurking enemy U-boats. Suddenly, the darkness was shattered by an overhead shower of rockets, shells, streamers and explosives. I couldn't believe that any enemy, no matter how desperate for a kill, would waste this much ammunition on a one-hundred eighty foot, unarmed Army vessel. At that moment, Sparks came running to the bridge and announced with pride that he finally deciphered the message: "Change course immediately You are heading into a naval practice firing zone!"

There was only one logical thing to do. Against all regulations, we switched on every light aboard: floodlights, running lights, anchor lights, deck lights until we looked like a floating Christmas tree. Firing stopped instantly. For a moment, silence. Then from all directions raging blinker signals from a dozen ships trained on us. Of course, we couldn't read them. We doused every light on board and with flank speed (whatever that is) did the prudent thing, moving out into the darkness in hopes we'd never be heard of again, but ready to meet whatever challenges that lay ahead.

Our chief engineer, Lt. Ronald Cuthburt, was a gentleman of the old South, an aristocrat with gently waved silver hair, a mien that we associate with "Gone With the Wind," complete with azure blue eyes that seemed to be tolerating the lack of couth that plagued the rest of us aboard FS344. In the officers' boardroom where we gathered for meals, Lt. Cuthburt discussed great books, classical music, Renaissance art, and the debilitating effect of contemporary literature on the developing mind. We took great pride in having a fellow officer who looked like Leslie Howard, bringing a touch of class to a group that had trouble determining which knife to use on the mashed potatoes. It was apparent to me that he well deserved his Superior rating—until I discovered that my chief engineer was into the sauce most of the time.

Lt. Cuthburt had previously completed rehabilitation to cure him of the vodka habit. It worked. Now he would touch nothing but bourbon with a twist. My first indication that there might be a problem occurred shortly after we left New Orleans: Lt. Cuthburt had forgotten to take on fresh water and our tanks were empty. When I questioned him, his explanation was so logical and included so many big words that I apologized for having mentioned the matter. It did create a problem for me. Now I had to make an unscheduled stop at Pensacola and I had never docked a ship this size in my entire thirteen-month career. It was six-thirty in the morning when for the first time I was bringing the FS344 alongside a pier. The dock belonged to the Frisco lines and there was a lone boxcar on a siding track that ran the length of the pier. Fortunately at that hour there was no one to witness my ship-handling ability. As I approached our mooring spot, I realized that this nine-hundred thirty-five ton ship was not my sixteen-foot sailboat on Lake St. Claire. Thirty feet from the dock, I ordered full astern but it was too late. The FS344 with a mind of its own continued on and the port side nestled against the dock with such force that the boxcar flew up in the air and came down six inches off the track. With some foresight, in the event there might have been a witness, I swung off with the tide and decided to take on water at Panama City where we were told it was sweeter and the piers friendlier.

We were ordered to Tampa and, while crossing the Gulf in mid-afternoon, the ship suddenly stopped. Dead in the water. No power of any kind could even flush the toilets or blow the whistle. The boys in the engine room were confounded. Then they discovered that every valve had been shut off. A call to the Chief was fruitless until we found his cabin door locked and Lt. Cuthburt inside sound asleep. When he felt he was going to pass out, he acted on the most conservative side of caution and shut everything down to be certain there would be no problems while he slept. Alongside the pier at Appalachacola, after an evening ashore, he mixed up the valves and opened a seacock by mistake. By morning the ship was resting on the bottom that, fortunately, was only two feet beyond our draft. On shore leave, Lt. Cuthburt usually would be delivered back to the ship by the MP's with a warning to me that if they ever saw him again I would be sailing without a chief engineer. In the bars he visited, Cuthburt would start out amiably reciting Shakespeare and dropping pearls of cultural wisdom that the beer and pretzel crowd seemed to enjoy. Then, after a few more bourbons on the rocks, Mr. Hyde would appear. With a withering look of distain, Cuthburt would label his fellow drinkers as louts without a shred of social grace and a disgrace to mankind, not worthy of a place in a society of good taste and fine breeding—like his. When the inevitable reaction occurred, he would challenge anyone in sight to a duel, with a choice of pistols or sabers. By this time the bar owner had called the police and the MPs would cart Lt. Cuthburt ingloriously back to his ship while he regaled them with threats to their careers, promising to have them broken back to buck privates and possibly court-martialed for disrespect and mistreatment of a prominent and honored military officer. The next morning Lt. Cuthburt would report meticulously groomed for breakfast, and in a most courtly manner discuss world events from the viewpoint of a dedicated scholar. He certainly brought a touch of class to our bacon and eggs.

Of course, I had to get rid of Lt. Cuthburt, but who would believe me? Each time I tried to have him reassigned, the review board would listen to my complaint, then interview this upstanding officer and suggest that I might be harboring a phobic antagonistic prejudice against Southern aristocracy. His appearance was so impressive that one member hinted that perhaps I should be investigated. I knew that if I could find evidence of liquor on board ship and attribute it to Cuthburt it would be his demise as Chief Engineer of the FS344. I conducted unannounced shakedown searches of the ship from stem to stern at all hours and never found an indication of his liquor supply. He was tolerant of our efforts to trap him. A condescending, but kindly smile that seemed to imply that we as children knew not what we were doing, but he would forgive. Years later, when I was giving up the ship, I uncovered his secret. Under my bunk lay four bottles of Canadian Club. I had never searched my own quarters. Our cabins were adjoining and it was a simple matter for Lt. Cuthburt to enter my room when I was on watch, extract a bottle, finish it off, toss the empty overboard, and then search for more valves to turn off.

Chapter Four

Montgomery Morgan - Eccentric, First Class

During a routine medical check up of the crew in New Orleans, I discovered that our first mate, Lt. Greg Dawson, was allergic to wool. Whenever Greg wore a government-issue wool shirt, his eyes would glaze over and he would stumble about the deck in a pathetic state of lost equilibrium. At the pier in Tampa, where we were taking on a cargo of essential war materials—three tons of Listerine and corn flakes destined for an air force base in Guatemala—Lt. Dawson fell off the gangway after putting on a pair of GI wool socks. At the time, he was wearing a life jacket that was unusual because no regulation we could find required life jackets to be worn while in port. Fortunately, Greg had thoughtfully left his wristwatch and wallet in his quarters that day. Shortly after being notified of the scheduled physical check-up, he began tripping over the three-inch high thresholds along the passageways whenever he was wearing wool trousers. It was evident that this was a serious allergy problem that could endanger those who were serving with him and possibly imperil the ship itself. The examiners agreed when the wool necktie Dawson was wearing during the interview caused him to fall from his chair. He was released from the military to return home and run his family's insurance agency. Our last word from him—he was entertaining clients on the ski slopes of Aspen. Wearing polyester, of course.

A message from the Army Transportation Corp informed us that 2nd Lt. Montgomery Morgan, replacement 1st mate, was to be brought on board at St Petersburg, Florida, and should be "extended every courtesy of your command." Usually orders read, "Officers will be expected to follow all military orders and carry out all assigned duties in accordance with the authority of his commanding officer." I was uneasy and wondered if young David Eisenhower might be joining our crew.

Our newest officer was to board ship at 1100 hours. It was mid-afternoon when a cab arrived on the Coast Guard pier and a scraggy figure emerged, peering into the sun through thick lens glasses like a peregrine about to devastate a flock of pigeons. When he hit the deck, he turned and saluted a seagull resting on the bow staff, ignoring the ensign proudly flying at the stern. For a moment I wondered if my father had been conscripted and sent to join me. This man was definitely beyond military age. His beaked nose, side-wise gait, and extensive overbite produced the combined appearance of a chipmunk peering through thick glasses. He spoke to me cheerfully and informed me he was Montgomery Morgan, the third, of Martha's Vineyard, ready to take on the responsibilities of serving as my first assistant. I had an uncomfortable feeling that with "assistance" like this there would be no shortage of handicaps at sea.

Before I could respond to his considerate offer, he asked if there was anyone available to take his duffel bag and suitcase to his quarters. Before I could explain that we were experiencing a shortage of personnel this season, Lt. Morgan stopped a passing crewmember, flipped him a five-dollar bill, and requested that his luggage be moved to his cabin. There was no hesitation. The seaman grabbed the bags and was off on a trot. I was beginning to feel my authority diminishing. The only rewards I had ever handed out were the occasional weekend passes when we were in port in recognition of someone's service above self as the ship was about to run aground.

I suggested that we talk over coffee so that I could be certain there had been no mistake in Pentagon orders or the possibility that this was an error and Lt. Morgan had really been assigned as a Chaplain.

He thought it a great idea and said he was eager to know more about me. The cook brought in two cups of coffee. Monty sent his back. "Not heavy enough," he said. "To be fit for drinking, coffee must be black as tar and strong enough to leave a permanent stain around the rim of the cup. I know that you Midwesterners like coffee-flavored hot water, but down east we need coffee you can cut with a knife. That's why we don't use spoons." He concluded his dissertation by announcing that he had brought with him his personal coffee pot and would brew his own beverage until the crew had learned to make and appreciate the real stuff. "A sailor can't stay awake on his watch unless he has coffee you can eat," he declared with the authority of the Ancient Mariner. "And now, Captain, what were you saying?" Actually, I hadn't said anything. But I was seething. How could I learn to tolerate a man I so thoroughly detested at the moment? Perhaps because he was always cheerful, even when the ship was close to foundering because Monty couldn't remember whether port is left, or is it right?

Montgomery Morgan was well beyond active duty military age, forty-four years old and not in top physical condition. He was lean, bony, and skinny with a tuft of wheat-color, unruly hair and coffee-stained teeth that pointed in all directions. His near-sightedness required that in one-on-one conversation you be nose-to-nose and prepared to receive a syllabic spray of moisture. Monty never "looked" at anything. He peered like a Dutch diamond-cutter squinting over a rare gem. When I asked for some explanation for his late-life military duty, he didn't hesitate to fill in all details that expedited his assignment as a marine officer aboard the FS344.

The Morgan family traced its roots back to the foundling fathers and every generation of Morgan's provided a Morgan to defend the nation that had brought so much of the good life to the dynasty.

Now it was Monty's turn to uphold the family honor, the valor first displayed with Washington at Valley Forge. There was a problem. Monty was too old. The Navy turned him down. When he applied for cadet pilot training, the Air Force thought he was kidding. The Army continued to say no until the family solicitor called their attention to the size of the Morgan contribution to the President's re-election campaign. With a nudge by the senator from Massachusetts, the Army was ready to deal. Monty would receive a commission as a Second Lieutenant but would have to sign a disclaimer absolving the government from any responsibility for his physical or mental well-being. This meant he would never see the inside of a veteran's hospital. The deal was done and the Morgan's honor was saved. The next question was what to do with the newly commissioned Second Lt. Montgomery Morgan. His application had mentioned that one of his college subjects was Marine Biology. The word "marine" to the land-oriented Army classification section meant that he must be a sailor. Also noted, Monty told them he owned a forty-two foot Alden cutter. This alone would indicate a healthy knowledge of seamanship. Monty had not mentioned that there was a paid crew of four keeping the vessel on an even keel while he on the stern deck savoring his Canadian Club with a twist.

The Boat Division of the Army was a logical assignment for a person with this background. At our first meeting, it was apparent that Lt. Morgan was a chain smoker. During our short discussion he went through a pack of

Winston's scattering matches and ashes the full length of the wardroom table. Punctuating his rhetoric with wild gestures, he propelled one of his burnt-out matches into my coffee. Monty must have had some Latin at Deerfield, his prep school. His conversation was sprinkled with Latin words and phrases that kept me more confused than informed. He referred to the officer wardroom as the *Calefactory*—from the Latin for heated room; his web GI belt was his "Cincture." Once, while we docked at New Orleans, he shouted at two prostitutes trying to come up the gangway, "*Egote expello!*" a phrase he explained would be more effective than "Get the hell out of here!" because it was once used in the Church during exorcisms or setting fire to heretics. Most annoying, Monty would shout "*Mea culpa! mea culpa!*" after casting off the launch before it had been made fast to the ship, or when he left the highly classified Navy-provided code books in a Charleston coffee shop. I learned that *mea culpa* meant "all my fault!"

Monty felt this was explanation enough for any near disaster he may have caused. At my initial meeting with him, I could tell he had not gone through officer orientation (of course, neither had I, but I did know which side of the collar rank insignia is worn, and that argyle socks are not regulation). The wide part of his necktie was neatly tucked into his shirt between the second and third buttons, but the narrow length hung down almost to his waist. The socks were a gift from his fiancée, Sylvia Raginfield of West Chester, who felt they would distinguish Monty from the run-of-the-mine defenders of the nation. Whenever there was an official inspection, we would assign two crewmen to dress Monty for the occasion.

Sylvia, his intended, had been selected as his bride-to-be by the two families after a thorough background search of both parties to be certain that the joining would be a match made in heaven, according to Dun & Bradstreet. Always the gentlemen, Monty told Sylvia there could be no marriage until after he returned from the battlefield. It would be unfair to leave her a grieving, but wealthy, widow. Apparently Monty did not want to be recklessly impulsive in matters of the heart, for it was not until ten years after the war's end that I read in the New York Times a three-column review of the Long Island wedding of Montgomery Morgan to the lovely, but aging Sylvia.

My ship-handling was a long way from Admiral Halsey standards, but with Lt. Morgan at my side it became, on occasion, a matter of embarrassing incompetence--if not criminal. It was in Tampa that everything seemed to be in my favor--tide, wind, and weather. I was pleased to see a group of spectators on the pier ready to admire my seamanship. An opportunity to demonstrate with pride that the Army could produce officers equal to any Navy sea-going professional, I guided the ship gently toward the pier, placing the bow close to the huge mooring cleat on the dock, then rang the engine room for slow astern to swing us alongside the pier. Everything was going perfectly and I was ready to step out on the open end of the bridge and take a bow--then the CRASH.

At sea, wartime regulations require lifeboats to be slung outboard from the davits to facilitate emergency launchings if necessary. Of course, in port the lifeboats are retracted inboard for docking. I had instructed Lt. Morgan, as we entered Tampa Bay, to bring in the starboard side lifeboat to prepare for docking. I had forgotten that Monty had trouble with starboard and port—like zig and zag, he had zigged when he should have zagged. As I lay the ship alongside the pier, I converted what had been a first-class lifeboat into a cord of questionable firewood, now hanging from the davits.

The crowd applauded. Best show they had seen since a Navy Hell Fighter landed at the Coast Guard station with its wheels retracted. Monty was chagrined, but not for long. After a couple of *"mea culpas,"* he suggested it would be prudent in the future to use right and left rather that the pretentious Naval expressions of port and starboard--although admitting that on some occasions he had problems with right and left. I told him that if the Army tried to take the cost of the lifeboat out of my pay, it was he who would be nailed to the wall until he covered it. Snuffy, our latrine lawyer, came to the rescue. He pointed out that two weeks earlier a minor hurricane in the Gulf had endangered a couple of our ships. With some of Snuffy's creative entries in the log, we could document our presence on the edge of the disturbance and the destruction of one of the lifeboats.

Various ports of call, ranging from Charleston, SC, to Central America and the Panama Canal, served as mail stations for the crew. In addition to letters, most of us received those welcome care packages from home--crumbled chocolate chip cookies, warm knit gloves for the tropics, money belts, and birthday cakes that metamorphosed into a questionable mass of gelatinous pudding. Monty's package was different. At our first stop at Charleston, there awaiting him was a case of Dom Perignon champagne and six cans of caviar. When I told him he wasn't allowed to bring anything alcoholic aboard, he was terribly disappointed, but in his generous way gave the champagne to a Salvation Army band playing on the pier. He informed the Salvation Army Captain that it was sparkling spring water from the Abbey of Dom Perignon in southern France, and that it was very appropriate to serve at prayer meetings. The Captain accepted it gratefully.

As First mate, Monty was expected to be navigating officer. We would work together as a team that occasionally resembled a comedy act, Monty at the chronometer and I on the wing of the bridge with the sextant. Upon my shout of "mark", Monty would note the time and then we would dive into those mathematical publications thoughtfully placed aboard by the Navy that assumed we knew the difference among those confusing titles of H0111, H0114 and H0112— books of numbers that would never be best sellers.

By the time we came to an agreement, it was usually an hour later than the observed time, so we always seemed to know where we had just been. Monty devised a one-out-three method that proved to be our most reliable. We would make three observations and the one out of three that indicated we were on water was the one we accepted. It was interesting the number of times Las Vegas showed up, which we knew could not be correct. Later, if we were in a hurry to know where we were, Monty came up with a procedure that was sure-fire. If we sighted another ship on the horizon, we would steam over to it and ask where we were. Sometimes Monty would have to toss over a can of his caviar if the informant was reluctant to reveal what surely was public information.

Monty was very popular with the crew, particularly at Christmas when he gave each member a twenty-five dollar war bond. I received a bottle of his champagne that now came aboard with vinegar labels in place of Dom Perignon. There was no problem a Morgan couldn't solve. Although generous in many ways, Monty had inherited the penurious attributes of the clan that had made the family a financial factor to be reckoned with. During a refitting period in Mobile, Alabama, Monty and I went ashore to have a dinner at one of the city's gracious old downtown hotels where, after the lifeboat incident, Monty was trying to make amends by picking up our tab. While walking through the lobby, he felt the Morgan instinct suddenly come into play; Monty left me and ran over to a bank of public telephones to check the return coin slots. He returned with a look of triumph to show me thirty-five cents in hand. I had a feeling that at this moment his father was doing the same thing back in New Port, Rhode Island, checking every public phone on Narragansett Bay.

My only real embarrassment that night occurred when the maitre d' noticed that Monty wasn't wearing socks. He might be different, but he was our eccentric.

A minor subject in Monty's education was entomology. Bugs fascinated him and he insisted that all insects have six legs—not four as Walt Disney would have us believe. Like all ships, the FS344 was infested with cockroaches and we had to undergo fumigation whenever we hit port with the right facilities.

After each fumigation, we were free of insects for about three days, and once again those indestructible cockroaches would hand us our socks when we opened our lockers. Other ships remained free of vermin for several weeks, but not the FS344. It was a mystery until we discovered that Lt. Morgan was harboring a small colony of cockroaches he removed from the ship during fumigation and returned to his quarters when the quarantine was lifted.

It was suddenly clear: we had a bug-bootlegger. Monty confessed. Said he couldn't bear to witness the destruction of this sturdy species and only wanted to preserve a few for his continuing study. We gave him a choice, either debugging or keel hauling—or, worse yet, we would ship a box of cockroaches to the Morgan mansion with his compliments.

We were at anchor about a mile off shore at Carabelle, Florida when a launch carrying a pair of wildly gesturing Greek nationalists came alongside to deliver privates Aristotle Thalis and Leondro Mattaxis as replacements for two of our seamen, Earl Putnam and Wayne Lawson, who were so prone to sea sickness that the sound of a flushing toilet would send them to the rail, on the leeward side, of course, even when the ship was secured to the pier. These guys were not faking. In an effort to get a transfer, they had volunteered for service with the paratroopers for duty behind enemy lines--anything to get off this insidious hunk of iron that tormented them day and night by moving up and down, even when at anchor, and left them the color of unripe olives.

In heavy seas, most of us experienced seasickness and, for short periods, wished we were dead. But for Putnam and Lawson, the *mal-der-mer* had become chronic. In storms, our bosun mate would lash the pair to the nearest stanchion to keep them from leaping overboard. However, had I known what I was exchanging them for I might have elected to take my chances and ply them with Mother Sill's seasick pills whenever the sky turned gray. Storms have always been part of a sailor's job description. I assumed that meant enduring uncomfortably rough weather conditions, without complaint. I discovered quickly that duty aboard a two-hundred-foot vessel on a savage sea could be close to the apocalypse.

In our first big storm, I was probably more scared than anyone else, but felt that I had to look nonchalantly competent while being tossed from one bulkhead to another. None of us farmers had ever imagined that waves could be so high, higher than the masthead and with the solid punch of an out-of-control Joe Louis. Each time the bow met those brick walls of water, the ship seemed momentarily to come to an abrupt stop, shudder briefly, and then plunge into the next rolling mountain. We would wonder how much longer the FS344 could hold together under this pounding of dropforge intensity.

From the bridge, the bow appeared to be disappearing forever into a water-filled canyon, and, in answer to our split-second prayers, slowly emerge shaking off rivers of water like a surfer ridding his hair of ocean brine. Storms lasting more than two days meant no food preparation, not that anyone was interested in eating. The racket of unsecured objects flying about the quarters revealed how unprepared we were for rough weather. On one occasion we found Monty Morgan locked in the walk-in cooler and eating ice cream.

"I wanted to be certain the food stores were stowed securely," he explained. "In seas like this we can't have the frozen peas rolling all over the deck. Very hazardous, you know."

"How long were you planning to test the ice cream?" said Second mate Lt Baldwin, always a little envious of Monty's wealth and critical of his seamanship. "Until the butter scotch brittle was gone?"

Monty ignored the sarcasm: "Somebody shut the door and I was locked in. Only thing I could find that would provide energy enough to sustain body heat was the ice cream. By the way, someone should check out the pistachio nut-those nuts are beginning to taste a little rancid."

I was upset about the extra work he had caused for the crew. "We've been searching the ship for more than three hours. Lt Cuthburt said he hoped you had been swept overboard."

Monty looked hurt. "Captain, sons and husbands all over the world are dying for their country. If I had been chosen to lay down my life for America, in whatever manner, I would have accepted my fate with honor and pride, a small price to pay for the freedom hundreds of thousands are striving to preserve. Also, this isn't a bad place to ride out a storm. Very little pitching, but bring warm clothes."

Lt Baldwin, anxious to get in another pitch, said, "Can you picture what a glorious death you might have had? If the cook hadn't come down to get a couple of salami rings for emergency feedings you would have been as stiff as a frozen dinner by morning."

"*Mea culpa, mea culpa,*" said Monty Morgan.

Corporal Earl Putnam was at the wheel during a storm so severe the starboard lifeboat was ripped from its davits. During a heavy sea a ship usually "quarters the waves," heading into each one at a forty-five degree angle as a compromise between wallowing in the trough and the bow-shattering force of a head-on sea. I had just snapped my lifeline to the bridge rail when I realized the ship was swinging off course. I rushed to the pilot's house and found it empty. No one at the wheel. I screamed for someone to take over the helm and then went looking for the missing quartermaster, Earl Putnam. I found him below, stretched out on a companionway deck and looking like a marinated cadaver. Trying to be heard above the storm, I yelled.

"Earl Putnam, you have deserted your post and imperiled the safety of the ship! This is a capital offense and you could be court martialed and possibly hanged from the yardarm." *I didn't know if we had a yardarm, but the expression sounded nautical.*

At this moment a sluice of water came rushing down the passageway causing me to lose balance and deposited me in a prone position nose-to-nose with Corporal Putnam. He opened his bleary eyes and in a mumbling voice was all sympathy for my position.

"It's okay, Captain," he said. "Don't be ashamed. Better men than us have gone down with their ships. You and I will stay right here until this tub sinks and puts us out of our misery."

It was then that chief Engineer Lt. Cuthburt emerged from a passageway door and stumbled over us and joined the heap of accumulating bodies sloshing in a rushing stream of salt water. Cuthburt was indignant. "Captain, your place is on the bridge during a storm, and not wallowing around in an enclosed space with a drunken seaman. Besides, officers should never fraternize with enlisted personnel." Cuthburt, on occasion, could be arrogantingly stuffy and this was one of those times.

"Go back to your engine room," I ordered. "This man is not drunk. I'm trying to place him under arrest even though he is deathly sick and wants to die. He doesn't seem to understand that he could be hanged or shot, or something for his offense."

Corporal Putnam, still flat on his back, continued to mumble. "We can all die together—there's no rank in heaven."

After Putnam and Lawson volunteered for the most hazardous duty the military could offer, provided it was not on water, court-martial charges were dropped and we prepared to welcome our share of the Greek maritime service as replacements.

Aristotle Thalios and Leondro Mattaxis were small, lean, and emotionally wiry, continually waving their arms to punctuate their limited English. Coming up the gangway, they were gesturing wildly as they argued who would get the upper bunk in the crew's quarters. When the axis powers invaded Greece, any Greek ships in American waters were seized and interned. Crews were given the option of being returned to their homeland, or, if they wished to remain in America, joining the U.S. Army. Aristotle and Leondro had seen the girls on the streets of New York, and unanimously decided that this country needed the Greeks for comfort on the home front. They would enlist in what ever it was.

During my initial conversation with them, I asked about their understanding of the obligations expected of them and were they ready to defend the integrity of the worthy FS344.

Leondro waved both arms above his head. "We no fighters. Aristotle and I, we lovers." And, with thumb and index fingers pressed together he threw an imaginary kiss toward the overhead.

This was a shocker. Off balance for a moment, I said, "Wait a minute, men. This is the U.S. Army. I don't know about Greece, but this sort of life style is not allowed in the military Service. Everyone on the FS344 has to be, you know, all the same. Know what I mean?"

Aristotle picked it up at once. "No, no," he exclaimed "I no love Leondro. Leondro, sometimes he hates me. Sometimes he no pay money he owes me. I kill him someday. We love girls. We make many girls very happy. Better than fighting. Except when husbands find out."

I was relieved. "What about your wives? You must have wives back in Greece?"

Leondro jumped in "No wives. We no married. We, like you say, free-lancers. We make many girls happy, wives, too. Not just one. Ship will stop in many ports?"

Private's Aristotle Thalis and Leondro Mattaxis were trained Merchant Marine seaman but after watching them thrash about wildly on the FS 344 I began to understand why the Greeks had so many historic problems on the Aegean Sea.

Everything was a crisis. The first time Aristotle participated in a docking procedure he tossed a heaving line to an individual on the wharf who appeared willing to handle our mooring lines. It was a good toss but he had neglected to fasten the standing end to the hawser to be hauled ashore. The result was a bewildered guy on the dock holding a free line and wondering if it were a gift, while the bow of the ship determined not to settle in its intended berth, began swinging out into the current.

Chapter Five

The logical solution to Aristotle was to scream at Leondro and scathingly accuse him of forgetting to secure the line. Not to accept blame gracefully, Leondro began waving his arms and shrieking that Aristotle was the victim of an ancient Thessalian curse that caused him to look and act like an idiot. All this while I was yelling from the bridge to get another line ashore before the tides took us back to sea. By the time the emotional finger-pointing concluded, we were in mid harbor, completely out of position for docking. It wasn't a complete loss. Two girls on the pier were eagerly waving at Aristotle and Leondro who responded by breaking into the steps of an ancient ceremonial Greek dance on the foredeck. The Coast Guard officer who had assigned us our berthing space stood on the dock, shaking his head and lamenting the day the Army had been allowed to participate in marine operations. It was a day of infamy for the hallowed traditions of the United States Navy. Worse yet, ships like the FS344 had been entrusted with the highly classified codebooks for naval operations. How would we ever win this war? It wasn't until during an informal inspection by Army brass that I learned the real expertise of Leondro and Aristotle.

Ships of our size were items of meddling curiosity to land-based Army people whose exposure to anything waterborne was limited to pontoon boats and Higgins landing craft. Whenever we were in port reasonably close to an Army installation, the local commandant would issue vague orders for an inspection of our vessel. That meant he and his staff wanted a boat ride. Private Snuffy, our invaluable guardhouse lawyer, developed a procedure that discouraged some of this fascination for the sea. It was usually late afternoon when we would weigh anchor and cruise a few miles in open water to satisfy our blue-ribbon guests. There was always a mild ground swell that would keep the ship gently rising and falling as we headed into the sunset. The inspection team would have just finished a free dinner on board and be out on deck, leaning on the rail, beating their chests and declaring how much salt water and the freedom of the open sea meant to them. The nearest most of them had ever been to water was inspecting Lister Bags on the post bivouac area. At this moment, Snuffy, now off duty, would sidle close to them at the rail and began a friendly conversation about life at sea. Then reaching into his pocket, he would pull out a specially prepared juicy lamb sandwich. As Snuffy continued to talk in his hypnotizing Oklahoma drawl, juice from the lamb fat would begin to dribble from the sides of his mouth. Always eager to please, Snuffy would offer to get a similar sandwich from the galley for his companions at the rail. The offer was always declined. As the undulating sea continued to raise and lower the ship gently, our guests would one by one excuse themselves from Snuffy's conviviality and explain that reports had to be completed, or that the sea air had made them sleepy. By the time we returned to anchorage around midnight, most of the inspection group would be stretched out on wardroom benches to catch up on the needed sleep so deserved by military men whose dedication to duty kept them at the officers' club far beyond closing time. After Snuffy's hospitality, we seldom saw them again.

How to Stay Afloat Wearing Army Boots

Administrative headquarters for the water division of the Transportation Corps was Camp Gordon Johnston near Carabelle, Florida. There was no deep water there so it was necessary to anchor a mile off shore while taking on replacements or special equipment. After a couple of weeks at sea the crew looked forward to a day at anchor when they could relax and catch up on mail and laundry. We arrived at Carabelle on a Sunday morning, dropped anchor, and settled down for a day of do-nothing, after two weeks of twenty-four hour duty days.

It was noon when the message came out that Colonel Wilfred Margin, post commandant, was arriving, with staff, for a property inspection and would expect a demonstration of ship operation. This meant a boat ride and bad news for the crewmen who had just spent two weeks battling near-hurricane weather and were looking forward to a day of catch-up. Getting a ship underway is no turn-key operation. It meant the entire crew would be on duty until we returned to anchorage late in the day.

Snuffy advised that we remain calm in our assessment of the situation. He had spent his entire military career outwitting superiors and this was just another challenge.

When Colonel Wilfred Margin and party arrived at our anchorage, it was quickly apparent this was the culmination of a happy hour, more social then military. We had some trouble getting the Colonel safely from his launch and over the taffrail on to the deck where he fell to one knee and complained about an old war wound that had left him with a gimpy leg whenever near salt water. Lt. Cuthbert, our chief engineer, mysterious produced a glass of iced tea that turned out to be straight Canadian Club. He suggested that a cool drink would relieve the tension in the Colonel's ailing leg if accompanied by a short period of rest. The Colonel downed the "iced tea" without comment and we gently eased him into the captain's bunk for a deserved afternoon's nap. Accompanying the

Colonel were four uninterested staff officers and a comely young civil service worker named Monya, the Colonels "secretary." It appeared that Monya's dedication to serving involved more than just taking dictation. She had no trouble leaping over the taffrail. Leondro and Aristotle immediately rushed to her side, providing as much assistance as they would an 80-year old lady crossing Fifth Ave in Manhattan. Leondro offered lemonade. Had she accepted, I don't know where he would have found the lemons. " Very warm day," Leondro said. "Beautiful lady should have cool drink. Leondro happy to get drink for her."

Aristotle, not to be out-performed, dashed below and returned with a small orchid plant he had lifted from a florist in Panama City. "Aristotle think orchid beautiful until he see you. Now orchid is nothing. Take it I will never be happy with it now."

Embarrassed, but pleased with all the attention, Monya disentangled herself and went below to check on the Colonel. "The poor dear, he works so hard. He never should have tried to leap over the tennis net last week," she said. "He should have a disability pension, but he's so valuable to the war effort."

By this time the Colonel was fast asleep, dreaming of the day he might make brigadier. The four aides recognized what we were doing, and to keep them busy we rigged a sail on one of the lifeboats and sent them off sailing around Dog Island. They loved it. The rest of us returned to our afternoon of rest and rehabilitation. Monya was missing but it was assumed she was with the Colonel applying cold compresses to his troubled brow.

About 1830 hours, the four aides returned with the lifeboat, all covered with brine but pleased with their ability to handle small craft in choppy seas. The Colonel was now stirring and stumbled out on deck. Someone of his staff asked if he enjoyed the cruise and did the ship pass muster now that we were back at anchorage. With serious mien the Colonel began searching his memory of the afternoon and finally said, "The ship handling was well performed, but the effectiveness of the stabilizers was not sufficient to prevent excessive and uncomfortable rolling. Quarters were clean and comfortable. The crew seemed competent and made every effort to accommodate the inspecting team. I question the condition of a lifeboat that appears to be rigged with a spar and sail. Not in accord with regulations. Later I will review the notes made by my secretary and prepare a more comprehensive report. By the way, where in the hell is Monya?" He was beginning to get a little testy and we were eager to see him back in the launch heading for shore.

Then things began to unravel. Lt. Baldwin pulled me aside and whispered, "We just located Monya. She's in the forecastle bunk with Leondro. They're making love like crazy, and Aristotle is standing by saying that if he doesn't get his chance he wants the orchid plant back." This was alarming news.

"For your sake and mine, get her ass back up here on deck right now!" I ordered. "Make sure she has on all her clothes. If the Colonel finds out we've seduced his girl friend we can all plan on serving as mess sergeants on the Italian front. To hell with Aristotle's orchid. Throw the damn thing overboard."

Baldwin hurried off to handle his delicate assignment while I informed the Colonel that his secretary had found the rough seas he mentioned in his report a bit discomforting and had been resting up in one of the bunks. She was now freshening up and would be ready to leave momentarily. The Colonel grumbled about a delay. "She's a very faithful secretary," he said. "A little weak on spelling, but very morale building when my responsibilities seem overwhelming. Always good in tight quarters."

Just then, to my relief, Monya showed up, looking happily at ease but without the orchid plant. "Found the sea a little too rough for you?" said the Colonel.

Monya smiled sweetly. "It was kind of choppy but the up and down motion was very pleasant."

The Colonel saluted the ensign and stepped smartly off the aft deck onto the launch. Then it happened. Monty Morgan, while handling the bow painter of the launch, spotted a green heron alighting on the ship's signal mast. With a cry of elation, he dropped the line and pointed at this rare sight. The bow of the launch swung with the current away from the hull and Colonel Wilfred Margin stepped into the sea.

All my past trespasses flashed before me as I tried to remember the proper form for the sign of the cross. The Colonel rose to the surface sputtering and cursing and threatening summary execution for the responsible party. A bosun chair was quickly dropped, landing on top of the thrashing victim. During the struggle, the Colonel lost his hat with the scrambled eggs so beautifully displayed. We managed to haul him back on deck, looking like a recently harvested sponge. Lt. Baldwin found a fatigue jump suit to replace the Colonel's uniform. The Colonel insisted on transferring his rank insignia and campaign ribbons to it.

Monya was at his side to comfort him, telling him how brave he looked in what could be shark-infested waters, then moved quickly out of sight while the rest of us groveled on the deck and begged forgiveness. The moment of truth came when Monty Morgan stepped up to the Colonel and said, "It was all my fault, sir. I hadn't seen a green heron since prep school at Deerfield. When this one landed on the flagstaff, I momentarily forgot my responsibility for your well-being. I knew the second I let that line go that I was putting at risk the life of one of America's true patriots, and that for the rest of my life I would regret this lapse of judgment, and that I was jeopardizing the outcome of this glorious cause that has brought us together on this occasion."

With an incredulous look at this near-sighted apparition of a chicken hawk, the Colonel bellowed, "Who in the hell are you?"

"Montgomery J. Morgan the third, late of Martha's Vineyard, Newport and Nantucket. Palm Beach during the inclement months--at your service, sir."

I had known that the Margin family ran a small seafood distribution business in Brunswick, Maine, but I was unprepared for Colonel Margin's reaction to the scion of the Morgan dynasty. For an instant the look of fury that struck terror in the hearts of young enlisted personnel seemed frozen, then slowly began to soften, changing to an impression of a Father Flanagan addressing a youth rally of under privileged boys.

Smiling, he said "Of the Booth Morgan Lobster cartel at Booth Bay?"

"The same," said Monty, "but just a minor part of the family operation. Timber is getting to be a real profit center for us. But, of course, lobster and crab will always be with us, for sentimental reasons. My great-great-grandfather was a lobsterman at Booth Bay in his youth and never forgot his seafood origins. Even from his yacht on Narragansett Bay, Granddaddy would occasionally drop a pot overboard. Said it was to remind him that he once worked with his hands. Never caught anything, of course, but we found out later that bootleggers on his payroll would fill those traps with booze from off-shore, and Montgomery Morgan, the first, would recover those pots on his next trip to Newport. Said it was more profitable than lobsters. But you and I know." Monty confided to the Colonel, "It takes a lot of little people to keep the big guys going. Without the small distributor doing all the work, it would be pretty tough for the Morgan's to keep that bottom line growing."

With a look of fawning admiration, Colonel Margin began to apologize to Monty for causing him so much anguish by falling in the drink. "Mighty clumsy of me," he said. "It's that gimpy knee. Monya always admired the way I used to leap over tennis court nets. By the way, where is Monya? Time for us to get going. Mrs. Margin always gets upset when I am late. Lt. Morgan, I want you as my dinner guest at the officers' club next time you're in port. You hear, now?"

Monya reappeared with a self-satisfied smile, ready to board the launch that we had now clamped to the ship's side with four grappling hooks. As it moved away, the Colonel tossed a friendly salute and Monya triumphantly waved the orchid plant above her head. Aristotle, at the port rail, looked exhausted.

Chapter Six

It was a day that was ending well. I found Monty on the bow with a pair of binoculars, searching for more green herons. "Lt. Morgan", I said, "get up to the chart room and record today's events in the log. Make it sound logical. Someday, somebody may read the thing. Also, keep in mind I don't give a damn how many lobster pots you may have on the bottom of Booth Bay. Until Emperor Hirohito blinks, you're still a caveat on the FS344!"

It was on the night of December 31, 1942, when the FS344 sank its first ship. Unfortunately, it was one of ours--or one of our friends, an Ecuadorian banana boat. It was about 2330 hours when we cleared the sea buoy and were entering the channel leading toward Tampa Bay, on the range and feeling secure that by midnight we would be at the dock in St Petersburg and ready to greet 1943. Range lights consist of two beacons, one far inland on a high elevation and the lower light at the water's edge. When both lights are lined up, one above the other, the most nervous ship's captain can feel confident that he is in the center of the channel and well away from shoals or shallow water as he approaches land. Conversely, an approaching vessel heading out to sea and also on range can feel equally assured that he, too, is in the center of the channel, well away from danger--unless there's an approaching ship on range and heading toward port with a skipper determined to take his half out of the middle. It is important at this point to be sure not to zig when you should zag.

We spotted what appeared to be a floating lumber yard at the same time we heard the voices of a joyous Latino chorus lustily singing a medley of central American folk tunes that seemed to include lots of dirty words. Lt. Baldwin sounded a long blast of our horn, signaling we were swinging to the right. Not to be intimidated, the Ecuadorians turned to their left and began hurling insults that implied we were of doubtful parentage. It was a hypnotizing moment for all of us as we watch this looming two-hundred fifty tons of weathered cord wood, under full sail, glide across our bow.

It was a depressing sound, like several hundred rail fences being turned to immediate kindling. We had struck the banana boat amidships and sliced more than half way across its beam. It was now hanging on our bow like an exhausted swimmer clinging to a slippery channel buoy, then slowly dropping off and beginning to give up. Not wanting to get wet, the crew of the doomed vessel began climbing over our port bow like a band of pirates intending to give no quarter. A murderous-looking crew determined to avenge the loss of their leaky home away from home.

Lt. Baldwin, fascinated by the scene, shouted, "Look, its Errol Flynn!" One of the uninvited invaders was carrying a knife between his teeth and appeared to be ready to make the gringos pay dearly. Their captain was having some difficulty standing erect, but implied with threatening gestures that the honor of his ship and country had been violated and that only unconditional surrender would be accepted. This was a situation not covered in the Naval Watch Officers Guide I had been studying since finding a battered copy in one of the lifeboats. Monty Morgan with his thick lens spectacles askew, had been watching the developing events with an open mouth that suggested he might be contemplating writing a check to cover the loss.

"Get the forty-five pistol from my cabin!" I ordered. "We've got to defend ourselves before we become prisoners of an allied nation." Monty hesitated for a moment, then headed below to bring up the forty-five caliber, overweight pistol I had been issued when I took command of the FS344. Because I had never fired anything more lethal than a Daisy Air Rifle, this bulky handgun always intimidated me. I kept it in my cabin on a shelf, and in my worst dreams I would see it falling to the deck, accidentally firing and shooting me in the foot.

Now was the occasion to prove my mettle as a fighting man, defending government property as well as avoiding captured by a friendly country. When Monty finally reappeared back on deck he was carrying a pie plate upon which rested the government issued weapon—in six pieces! Monty, ill at ease and with some indication of embarrassment, explained "I field-stripped and cleaned it for you this afternoon. Thought you would be pleased that I recognized the poor condition it was in. Problem was I couldn't put it back together and I planned to have one of the enlisted men reassemble it tomorrow—they're trained in that sort of thing, you know."

I was astounded. "My God, Monty, you've taken our only means of defense and broken it down to its basic parts! Do you want to volunteer to duke it out with these wild bongo-playing maniacs?"

Monty looked hurt. "What about the fifty-cal machine guns on the bridge?" "I was pretty good when we were shooting seagulls last week."

"They're set so they can't be trained to fire down on the deck," I said. "Guess the Army never intended for us to be shooting our own crew. Besides, you never hit a single seagull. That was a fish-loaded pelican stupid enough to fly across your line of fire. You never saw it. Monty, I'm going to remember this when I make out your fitness report next month, if we're still around where anyone cares."

Our laundered survivor guests were now advancing toward us and shouting unintelligible Latin phrases that sounded like, "Now you're going to get it!" I had to make a decision. Would we hurl the dismembered pieces of the forty-five at them, or would we negotiate and offer to buy their sunken hulk with Monty Morgan's no-limit credit card?

Suddenly, like the sound of a rescuing US Cavalry charge, we heard a loud, clear, cultured voice with a tinge of Southern hospitality across the clamoring horde. "It's midnight! Happy New Year, everybody! Let's celebrate!"

It was our alcohol-inclined chief engineer, Lt. Ronald Cuthburt, standing tall on the hatch of number one hold, waving four bottles of his precious Canadian Club bourbon. It was a beautiful sight.

I was bewildered. Where did Cuthburt stow his cache of liquor? (We had just searched the ship from idiomatic stem to stern.) And why did he feel this was an appropriate time to have a party? For a moment there was silence. The Ecuadorians stared at this figure offering to share top quality booze with an unruly band of hostile boarders. Then there was a shout of exuberant joy and goodwill as our moment-ago attackers decided a party was the way to go. The captain of the lost ship, after being helped to his feet, insisted on proper protocol by demanding the first swig before passing the bottles down the line to the crew. His first toast, of many, was touching: "Americans good friends. Come to Ecuador, I will give you many bananas—my sister, too. Very pretty."

The congeniality taking hold was tempting to our own crew who felt the events of the evening entitled them to a share of the festivities. On the advice of Snuffy, I confined everyone not on watch to quarters. No sauce sampling for them. Snuffy knew that later we would be required to throw a few stones, and we must be without sin.

Word of the crash had already reached the coast guard station at Tampa. When we arrived at the pier, there was a delegation of port officials on hand ready to evaluate the situation and make an initial assessment of responsibility. The Ecuadorians were still singing their bawdy folk songs. Some needed assistance to traverse the gangway. The Captain required a litter and complained bitterly about a lost box of Cuban cigars. Our crew, sober and serious (with the exception of Lt. Cuthburt, now locked in his cabin), stood at attention as they bade farewell to their convivial guests, survivors without rancor. Our officers expressed deepest sympathy to Ecuadorian envoy for the loss of so fine a banana boat. He muttered something about justice and a possible two million-dollar settlement if we expected the bananas to keep coming—a paltry sum in view of this wanton destruction of the flower of the Ecuadorian merchant service.

There was of course, a court of inquiry to determine who really zigged when they should have zagged. I had visions of things going wrong, particularly the two million dollars being assessed against me, which at my pay rate would assure me of uninterrupted military service for the rest of my life, through regular payroll deduction.

By the time the date of inquiry was set, most of the banana boat crew had disappeared. The Captain had been undergoing detoxication and treatment for gout. He could remember nothing about the crash other than his loss of "very expensive box of Cuban cigars. Must have new cigars or I say bad things about USA."

We were cleared. The opinion was that the Ecuadorians were operating under the influence of something other than coffee and that we aboard the FSC44 had performed responsibly.

Our cook, who had basic training, put the forty-five pistol back together for us.

As an expression of my appreciation to Lt Cuthburt for saving the day, I wrote to the DOD and submitted a request that a special commendation ribbon be awarded him for distinguished service above self for risking his life defending his fellow officers and protecting government property. A puzzled major at the Pentagon asked for a detailed explanation of the risk taken and a full description of the action involved. Snuffy advised me to forget it.

December 31, 1942—a night to remember.

Chapter Seven

Navigation equipage aboard an orphan Army vessel was not exactly state-of-the-art. Ours consisted of a magnetic compass, a sextant, a chronometer (with a 12-minute lag), and a set of Hydrograhic Office Tables – HO 111, 212 and 214, all complied by the WPA in 1932, and all involving algebra, calculus, and other long-forgotten high-school subjects. No radar, just being introduced on aircraft's carriers and battleships, no radio or satellite signals to pin point our position. Just our Boy Scout instincts to guide us in making an X on the chart and saying here we are.

    The only armament on board were two 50-calibre machine guns on top of the bridge and a formidable looking 40-mm gun on the bow. We had a problem with the fo'c'sle deck gun--there was no barrel. It was deep in the hold, crated and so heavy we had no way of bringing it up on deck. If we ever could hoist it in place, none of us had the ordnance expertise to install it. The swivel mount on the forcastle deck was threateningly impressive with two tractor-style seats and a pair of rotating control wheels which allowed a couple of eager operators to raise or swing the piece into position as it zeroed in on a hapless enemy--if only there had been a barrel.

A stiff canvas cover protected the mount and the gun was always in place with the portion intended to cover the barrel extended outward toward the potential target.

In each port we would ask Navy ordnance to install the displaced barrel but there was always some cop-out reason about the matter being an Army problem which could be handled at our next port of call. I was beginning to wonder whom we should fear most--the Navy or the Axis powers. The barrel never did get into place until we were in the South Pacific near the end of the war when a group of bored but sympathetic Sea-Bees took care of the problem. We rewarded them with a full case of toilet paper deeply appreciated because they were down to using pages from the USO supplied LIFE magazines.

During the required daily emergency drills, the alarm would be sounded and each crewman would rush to his designated post, grumbling and complaining about the inconveniences of war. Aristotle and Leondro were posted to mann the gun on the bow. Swinging the swivel mount and empty barrel cover in all directions, they reveled as they brought down imaginary Mitsubichi dive bombers and blew enemy torpedo boats out of the water. Singing excerpts from LaTravita, they were a beautiful sight.

But at dawn on the morning of October second, things were different. At sea, day breaks all at once. There isn't a dawn as we know it. One moment it's night, and the next it's day. Black to white in an instant. It was then we saw it—a grey, cigar-shaped German submarine surfaced five-hundred yards off our starboard quarter to recharge its batteries. The several crewmembers on its deck were more startled and scared than we were. I rang the alarm for general quarters (whatever that meant). Our crew piled out of their bunks, bitching about an army that would go through this daily chicken maneuver just to satisfy some over stuffed piece of brass in the Pentagon. Aristotle and Leondro skipped across the deck to their post on the forty-mm gun, swinging it in all directions until, seeing it for the first time, the stiff barrel cover pointed directly at the sub's conning tower. It was a shocker for our Greek peace lovers to be looking directly into eyes of the enemy. Aristotle fainted.

The submariners on deck realized that they were targeted in the sights of a gun capable of turning their sub's thin skin into a sieve. There was frantic scrambling as a German officer began screaming orders; horns blared, bells rang, and the five crewman dove through the conning tower hatch. It clanged shut and our sitting duck enemy went into a crash dive. In less than a minute, it disappeared below the surface with a wake that indicated a westerly heading. We made a hard turn to port and, at flank speed, headed east.

Today, I can picture a retired German U-Boat commander writing his memoirs, relating how close he came to being blown out of the water on an October morning in the Gulf of Mexico. Lt. Baldwin went below in the number one hold and painted a small Swastika on the wayward gun barrel, which he then X'ed out to symbolize our first victory at sea. It was a touching moment.

While delivering a small cargo of good conduct ribbons, swagger sticks, and Eisenhower field jackets to an Army cantonment at Charleston, SC, we were ordered to pick up a disabled Army tug-boat near Paris Island and tow it to a shipyard at Jacksonville. A simple assignment, we assumed.

Arriving at the area we discovered that the tug was some distance up the Coosawhatchie River, in water not navigable for a vessel of our draft. Aristotle and Leondro asked that they be allowed to take our launch up the river and bring out the disabled boat. Knowing that our two Greeks were trained seamen in the Greek merchant marine service and capable of small boat handling, I sent them on their way with a traditional Corinthian Orthodox blessing. The trip up river involved passing under two drawbridges which did not require raising because the launch had no superstructure. Finding the small tugboat was the easy part. Leondro expertly secured a towing bridal to the disabled craft and the trip down river began. At the first draw bridge, he gave no signal to raise the span. The launch cleared easily, but our Grecian seamen had forgotten about the super structure of their tow--a raised pilot house, two signal masts, a life boat on davits, and staffs at both bow and stern. As the launch passed under the span, the bridge tender rushed to the rail and shouted at Aristotle and Leondro, waved his arms and tried to warn of the disaster about to happen at the end of the tow line. Ever friendly, our gregarious Greeks waved back with an Ionian salute of fraternity. The two crewmen aboard the tug ducked below deck, reciting their rosaries and praying for everlasting life. The sound of the crash echoed along both sides of the river. Traffic on the bridge came to a standstill while spectators enjoyed the demolition on water. Leondro and Aristotle broke into unintelligible panic, screaming and pointing accusing fingers at each other. In a frantic attempt to stop the launchs forward motion, they managed to stall out the engine. Unfortunately, the tide was coming in, reversing the direction of the river; now the tow-er and the tow-ee were moving with the current back under the bridge for the second time. Before the engine could be restarted, the hapless tug completed a return trip under the bridge and the deck items that escaped destruction the first time were wiped out in this second try. With a cry of victory, Aristotle got the engine firing again and at full speed ahead yanked the tug back under the bridge for the third time. A jury-rigged staff with a distress flag at its peak, fashioned by one of the terrified crewmen, was taken out on this final trip under the bridge. The second drawbridge was no problem. The tugboat had now been cut down to a size that would comfortable pass through a storm drain.

    With a look of mission accomplished Leondro and Aristotle delivered to our side what appeared to be a Chinese junk after surviving a Pacific typhoon.

    After tranquilizing the two shaking crewmen from the tug, we immediately put them on a bus back to their base at

New Orleans. It seemed prudent to get any witnesses out of the area, fast. The shipmaster of the marine repair yard in Jacksonville was puzzled. After looking at the floating scrap yard I had brought him, he said, "They told me I'd be getting a disabled tug, but nothing like this."

"Enemy action," I said, and broke for cover.

How to Stay Afloat Wearing Army Boots

Chapter Eight

Lookout duty aboard ship is an assignment most sailors abhor. It is monotonous, boring, uncomfortable even in fair weather, and tends to produce a feeling of serving without purpose. Stationed at the foremost area of the bow, the lookout gets drenched by bone-chilling spray. The normal pitch of the vessel produces an up and down elevator motion that will induce seasickness in the hardiest of sailors. Assignment to lookout was like drawing KP duty at an Army reception center. Every well-trained soldier had a pocket full of reasons why he was not fit for responsibility so great.

When private Elwood Corbin volunteered for such duty on a permanent basis, everyone was pleased, although concerned about the judgment of anyone willing to fill a post shunned by sailors around the world since the Phoenicians plied the Mediterranean Sea. Private Corbin was not exactly Rhodes Scholarship material. After a couple of sessions at seamanship classes, Elwood learned to tie knots so well he had to be cut out of his shoes one night. As a wheelsman, he had trouble discerning right from left, and at command of "steady as you go" Elwood would drop the wheel and stand at attention.

We suspect that for the United States Navy it was John Paul Jones in 1784 who initiated the regulation that all ships underway must have a lookout in place. He probably devised the crow's nest where, high up on the main mast, the lookout could shout, "Land Ho!" whenever tops of palm trees appeared over a misty horizon. Today, the Navy requires the lookout to be at the bow rail ready to alert the officer of the watch to any obstacle ahead that might endanger the ship. Of course, the bridge being higher than the bow provides a view more expansive than any available to the lookout. By the time the lookout spots an endangering object, the officer on the bridge has already changed course because he saw it first. A cold, frustrating job usually assigned to a sailor in need of discipline.

Private Corbin's request was welcome but suspect. When I asked him why, he drew himself up to his full five-foot eight and said, "Looking out for the ship is a responsible job. Makes me feel important knowing that my shipmates depend on me. I've got sharp eyes and won't miss a thing. You wait and see. I will find things you never knew were out there. I will be the champion lookout of the world!"

With enthusiasm like that and because no one else would volunteer for the post, Elwood was not to be denied. As we left port, he stood proudly at the bow rail and peered into the spindrift and wind like a house detective searching for purloined towels, ready to alert the world to any perils that lay ahead.

The first watch was uneventful. No icebergs, no kamikaze pilots—nothing but wave after wave of brine washing over the foredeck. Then, on day number two we began to hear continuous reporting of foreign objects that were showing up on Elwood's visual radar:

"Empty beer carton two points off starboard bow."
"Friendly aircraft at three o'clock." That was the regular PanAm flight to Mexico City.

"Three porpoises under the port anchor. Oil drums floating half mile abaft the beam." Flock of thirty-two seagulls directly overhead."

As we left the Miami jetty one evening, Elwood reported in a booming voice "Raw sewage directly ahead. Three floating rubbers. Two look used."

In Tampa Bay as we passed a small drifting sail boat, Elwood reported: "Couple making out under awning on twenty-five foot sloop."

Initially, the crew looked forward with some amusement to Elwood's running commentary, but then began to find the never-ending reporting a bit annoying. One crewman complained that it was difficult to sleep during his off-watch because Elwood never stopped alerting the bridge that there was more than just water out there. When the complainant was offered the opportunity to serve as a replacement lookout, he elected to use earplugs.

Warrant Officer Mike O'Neil, Third Mate, tried to reason with Elwood. He suggested that he edit his observations down to the essentials.

Corbin stood at attention and quoted directly from the US Naval Seaman's Guide: "Lookouts are expected to report in a clearly audible voice to the officer of the watch all foreign objects or hazards that lay ahead, including any shipboard activity within sight which might impede the safe progress of the ship. It is also expected that after dark the lookout will report any unusual action which might occur on the deck area within his view."

W.O. O'Neil sighed. "Elwood, I want you to know that I don't agree with some of the crew who claim that you're the intellectual equivalent of an enema."

"Thank you," said Elwood Corbin, Lookout First Class.

The ship had, for all practical purposes, tuned out Corbin's tour-guide commentary until we left Brownsville, Texas. It was a moonless night around 2300 hours, and Elwood Corbin had just announced a shooting star at one-hundred forty-five degrees. Suddenly, he boomed, "A ghost is dancing on the number two hatch cover!"

Lt. Baldwin, officer of the second watch, was on the wing of the bridge sipping coffee and dreaming of his deteriorating insurance business back in Bristol, Connecticut, when the startling announcement of "ghosts" brought him back to the war and the Gulf of Mexico. Strapping on the empty forty-five calibre pistol, he rushed down to the deck-well ready to repel any spiritual boarder. Of course, he found nothing—just the slapping sound of the bow waves on a calm sea.

Elwood stood by his pronouncement: "It was all in white, running and leaping from one hatch to another."

"Why didn't you apprehend it?" said Baldwin. "You know a ghost isn't in our table of organization. Might have been a saboteur trying to plant a bomb and blow us out of the water."

"Couldn't leave my post," said Elwood. "Seaman's Guide says never leave assigned position, just alert the watch. Besides, I figured someone would catch the ghost cause I could see in the dark a couple of guys chasing it around until everybody disappeared."

When I relieved Lt. Baldwin at the end of the watch, he was perplexed. "Either we send Elwood ashore for some R&R or we have the ship exorcised," he said. When I questioned the crew, they responded with blank stares and complete ignorance of anything other than the normal shipboard routine.

There was an exception. Snuffy had a look of minor concern. I wondered how much he knew about the ethereal-- after all, he knew about everything else.

Sailors always look forward to a stop at Brownsville, Texas. It is on the border, directly across from Matamoros, Mexico, a far more interesting place for crewmen to spend shore leave than at the USO Canteen in Brownsville. Leondro and Aristotle said that Matamoros was like their hometown in Greece, but pleasure rates were higher in Mexico. Although they made many girls happy in Matamoros, it was expensive and they lamented the lack of true love. Price control was certainly needed if we were to maintain high morals among our Greek compatriots.

After we left Brownsville, our schedule called for stops at Corpus Christi, Mobile, and several other Gulf ports until four days later when we arrived at our base in Tampa.

Shortly before casting off, Leondro and Aristotle asked for a change in their sleeping quarters. They preferred a much less desirable area of the ship. The crew was quartered at the stern in a comfortable section aft of the dining area. The two Greek seamen pointed out that if they were moved to a small room in the forecastle that there would be more room for the remaining crewmembers in the aft section. It would be a sacrifice for the Greeks because quarters in the bow area were uncomfortable and seldom used.

The bow portion of the ship takes a continual beating. Trying to sleep there is difficult, particularly during heavy weather. The forecastle consists of three small rooms: the chain locker, the paint locker, and a small area with a pair of fold-down bunks. The offer to move to a place of few creature comforts was an expression of compassion for their fellow mates--or was it Greeks bearing gifts? The rest of the crew encouraged the change, pointing out it would make more room for them. Every one seemed unnaturally happy about the new arrangements.

During the four-day voyage across the Gulf, there was an encouraging display of compatibility among the crew. Morale was high, sociality increased. In an apparent effort to keep Aristotle and Leondro from feeling isolated, crewmembers off-duty would visit them in their cramped quarters at all hours. It was a happy ship. Although there was considerable deck traffic for Elwood to report, there was never another sighting of the ghost.

Finally we docked at Tampa. Lt. Baldwin was on afternoon deck watch when Leondro approached and informed him that a stern mooring spring line appeared to be chafing and might part at any minute. Baldwin went aft to investigate and found no problem. Returning quickly to the gangway, he spotted the two Greeks leaving the ship with an attractive Latino female clad in skintight jeans and a brief, lacy halter-top.

Baldwin yelled. "Halt!" But, to no avail. The trio seemed not to hear until he yanked out the empty pistol, aimed it in their direction and shouted again. "Halt, or I'll fire!"

This time, the Greeks heard and began talking at once. They explained that the young lady had just come aboard by mistake while looking for her brother.

Explaining that women were never allowed on a military vessel, the Greeks escorted her ashore. Baldwin said she must never make that mistake again. Very bad. He had not wasted eight years of his life as an actuary not to recognize a snow job.

"Stand fast," he commanded. "All three of you are under arrest. I'm calling the Captain."

Aristotle became deeply concerned. "Lydia's mother very sick. She waiting at home. Lydia must go to her now. She go now?"

Baldwin snorted. "How do you know her name is Lydia?" Then, turning to the comely prisoner he said, "Where does your mother live? Do you even have a mother? What are you doing here, as if I don't know?"

Lydia was not one to be intimidated. She tossed her jet-black hair in a provocative way, smiled, and rolled her almond eyes at the stalwart ex-insurance agent.

"Lydia mother in Mexico. Leondro, my friend tell me this is Matamoros. He never lie."

Leondro groaned. Lydia continued, "Never mind mother, she old. Lydia have many sisters. All pretty like Dolores Del Rio. Lieutenant like pretty girls? Sisters like strong lieutenants. Everybody be happy."

Lt. Baldwin tore his sight away from the tight jeans and turned to the would-be protectors of womanhood.

"You guys are in big trouble," said Baldwin. "Trying to smuggle illegal aliens into the USA is a capitol offense—and running a whorehouse on government property is even worse!"

When I arrived on the scene, the rest of the crew that had initially been attracted by the confrontation seemed to have disappeared. Only the three culprits and Lt. Baldwin remained on deck.

Baldwin summarized the situation. "What do you want to do, Captain? Put them in irons right now?"

Of course, we didn't have any irons, but the expression sounded nautical and I was proud of my first mate for using it.

"No, no," I said. "It's all very simple. We call the port authorities right now and turn them in for bringing illegals into the country. Simple as that."

Aristotle and Leondro were busy pointing at each other and disclaiming any knowledge of Lydia Gomez's existence.

I took some pride in having made this command decision so quickly, the mark of in-charge authority when others are floundering. The matter was wrapped up—until I felt the presence of someone at my side. It was Snuffy.

"Perhaps we shouldn't be so hasty," he said. "Could I have a word with you in the lee of the long boat?"

I wanted to tell him the matter was settled and to get back to his chipping and painting duties. Nevertheless, something from past experiences told me it would be prudent to listen.

We moved to a space between the launch and the rail. I waited for Snuffy while he place a pinch of Copenhagen in his left cheek. "This could be a little nasty."

"What are you talking about?" I said. "It's all cut and dried. They were caught with an illegal Mexican trying to take her ashore."

Snuffy spit over the rail. Finally, in that insufferable Louisiana drawl Snuffy said, "You've had this illegal girl aboard for four days, running a prostitution operation to keep the crew happy, and then to save your own skin you turn her in as an illegal alien?"

"Wait a minute!" I shrieked. "You know that's not true. This is the first moment I knew that the Latin bimbo existed."

Snuffy grinned. "I know it's not true and so do you. But what about the promotion hungry Feds among the Port people? Who do you think they'll believe when the Greeks finish telling their story? You know damn well Leondro and Aristotle aren't going to risk being shipped back to occupied Greece or throw themselves on the block when they've got a responsible CO to pick up the burden."

"I've got witnesses," I protested. "The crew knows I was unaware of any hanky-panky, every one of them!"

"Wait a minute," Snuffy said. "Every member of the crew, with the exception of Elwood, was buying time with Lydia. The Greeks were running a first class whorehouse with built-in motion. Prices were right, with a volume discount if you were up to it. They're all going to plead ignorant and pass the buck to you. Think about those home-office heroes in JAG who would wet their pants to have a service record showing that they nailed to the wall the CO of one of those detested Army ships."

"What about my officers. They'd support me."

Snuffy counted on his fingers. "You've got six officers. There are sixteen enlisted men. You're outnumbered, Skipper."

"What about you?" I said. "You didn't have anything to do with Lydia Gomez."

Snuffy took another pinch of Copenhagen, looked out at the seagull-covered channel buoy. "I'll take the fifth on that."

I was beginning to feel uncomfortable, but I knew that Snuffy always had a solution. "What do we do?"

"I know we're heading back to Brownsville tomorrow," said Snuffy. "Perfect for our plan. We confine

Lydia to her quarters, under guard of Elwood because he still thinks she's a ghost. Move the Greeks back with the rest of the crew. When we arrive in Brownsville, Lydia is escorted back to Mexico and we make believe it never happened."

"What about the Greeks?" I said. "They started all this. Can't let them come away with nothing more than a reprimand."

Snuffy had thought of that, too. "We canvas the crew and under threat of court martial make them tell us how much they spent for Lydia's favors and require Aristotle and Leondro to forfeit the full amount. We put that money in the crew's welfare fund and take them to Arnold's for dinner the next time the ship is in New Orleans." It all sounded so logical. Why didn't I think of it, instead of a guy who couldn't make corporal?

When we arrived in Brownsville our sister ship, the FS343, was there under the command of Charlie Harper. I worried my crew not to mention any part of our recent problems, which I would deny, of course, but it might spread rumors.

Because they had brought her aboard, I assigned Aristotle and Leondro the task of getting Lydia back into Mexico where they had discovered her. Two hours later they reported back, mission accomplished. Lydia was pleased that we had given her fifteen percent of the pot to help her get started in some reputable endeavor.

A week later we again met up with the FS343 in Galveston. Over a drink, Charlie Harper told me about some strange activities aboard his ship. Said his crew had started a card game in the empty number one hold behind some empty shipping cartons. Spent so much of their off-duty time at the game they were beginning to look wan and worn. Also, that one night a mysterious ghost-like figure wearing a diaphanous gown had been sighted flitting over the boat deck.

I suggested that for the welfare of his crew, he put more saltpeter in their food.

Elwood continued to look for ghosts. We never did tell him that it was Lydia in her "wedding gown" enticing the boys to a glorious fifteen-minute honeymoon.

How to Stay Afloat Wearing Army Boots

Chapter Nine

When I entered Military life, I met the great Fabian Murphy. We were among eighty-two uneasy recruits on their way to a future of indeterminate military service, some leaving the warmth of home for the first time, apprehensive and nervous—except Fabian. There was something about him, his carefree self-confidence and look of implied knowledge about all things that really mattered, that suggested this would be a good man to know and have on your side.

    At the rail station, the restless group, still in civilian clothes, waited to board the train that would wind through Durand and other small Michigan cities picking up additional draftees for eventual deposit at the Fort Sheridan reception center near Chicago. Physically, Fabian looked no different from the others: average height, wavy blond hair, and Irish blue eyes that expressed sincerity and tolerance for those who didn't quite understand the situation. If there was any concern about his future in a war-torn world, it was belied by an aura of over-confidence and clandestine authority that might cause some uneasiness in the long grey line of Army command.

    Like hens with their chicks, anxious selective service officials, border-collie style, were circling their charges making certain that none might decide before getting on the train that their country really didn't need them and wander away. As early evidence of his magnetism, a few of the recruits began to drift in the direction of Fabian Murphy, listening to his encouraging words about the perks and advantages of life in the Army, sounding like a veteran who had fought on every front from North Africa to Mandalay. Already he was a leader without uniform. There was no question in the minds of our handlers—Fabian was put in charge, a four-hour command position to deliver eighty-two men to the reception center.

I was older (twenty-seven) than the others and Fabian seemed to feel he could confide in someone close to his own age. I was flattered. He had been a salesman of questionable securities in a Boston bucket shop, peddling blocks of investment "opportunities" to visiting dignitaries to bean city. He was proud of a sale he had made to Bob Hope. Each day he would scan the newspapers and select the most prominent visitor to whom he would offer a once-in-a-lifetime financial opportunity. With Fabian's Irish chutzpah, he was always able to reach his target over the telephone, implying that he might be related to the chairman of The Federal Trade Commission. He was cool. If there was hesitation to put him through to the celebrity, he would admonish the staffer with "Don't have Mr. Hope call me back. I can't keep this offer quiet for more than an hour. When it breaks on the street, it will be gone in ten minutes. Frankly, I shouldn't have made this call. There are house clients who should have been contacted first-- but in view of Mr. Hope's patriotism, there is an obligation and I've got a conscience. I know he's busy and I'm sure there will be other opportunities to triple his investment in ninety days. Here's my number, if he wants to say hello."

Hope did call back and Fabian related to me, with pride, the pitch that became the summit of his boiler shop resume: "Mr. Hope, I have a limited numbers of shares of Essence of Apricot Pits, the newly discovered miracle elixir.

At risk to myself, I've been holding them for someone whose devotion to our country deserves recognition and a symbol of reward for true service above self. Too long the financial community of America has felt that people of substantial means, like yourself, should always give and not expect retribution in any form for the voluntary services they so unselfishly perform. I feel differently, which is why I've been holding these remaining seven thousand shares of Virgin Apricot Essence shares for you. Venture capitalists have been begging for them, but quick profit is their modus operandi; yours is unselfish patriotic service and deserves something more than just medals and ribbons. No, I cannot in good faith offer anything less than the full seven thousand shares. To offer you less would be an insult to your purchasing capability, and the richly deserved maximum return from this medical miracle, Essence of Virgin Apricot Pits.

"Please don't feel that you must accept this reward. Financial planners representing Mr. Bing Crosby called last week seeking a chance to buy in, but I'm holding them off. While Mr. Crosby is a fine and patriotic gentleman, your selfless contributions—promoting the sale of war bonds, and entertaining our troops overseas—outweigh the efforts of even Benny Goodman or Alice Fay. We will be pleased if you accept this token of our appreciation. You may instruct your management to mark your check to my attention. As we both know, the FSE requires full and immediate payment for security purchases. We're in no hurry, but they are. It's good to know that there are occasions when good people do win."

Shortly after leaving the station, one of Fabian's charges began quietly sobbing in his seat next to the window. Recently engaged to be married, he feared he would never see his intended again . . . or worse that he might receive a "Dear John" letter.

With the tone of a chaplain, Father Murphy began damage control:

"Your girl got engaged to you because she thought you were a great guy. There are plenty of 'great guys' back there who may tempt her, but, remember, there are no heroes on the home front. The real patriots and heroes are soldiers like yourself. When she reads about the coming invasion of Europe, you may not be there, but she will associate you in her mind with all those heroes getting their ass shot off. You may end up as a company clerk at a quartermaster depot in Iowa, but when you get home with all those ribbons—good conduct, unit citations, and all those other medals your company commander wanted for himself but had to include you to get his--you'll be General Patton in her eyes. Those homebound draft-dodger studs will look like garbage. If she likes you now, imagine her hot feelings when you get back. Better remember to take back a good supply of those Army issue rubbers with you. Save some money."

The kid brightened and said, "Thanks, Sarge," even though Fabian, like the rest of us, was still in civilian clothes. There was a feeling among a few that he was an undercover intelligence officer sent along to infiltrate the new recruits for the purpose of weeding out subversives. Actually it was his wheeling-dealing civilian life that kept him too busy to figure out how to beat the draft.

I was flattered that, after strolling the length of the railway car, he came back and settled into the seat next to me. He had discovered one of the men nipping from a pint bottle of bourbon. After confiscating the taboo beverage, Fabian severely lectured the recruit on the bad start he was making in the service.

"Don't you realize that alcohol is strictly forbidden in the armed forces at all times? Bringing that bottle with you could be on your record for life! For your sake I'm going to keep quiet, but if it's ever found out, this offense could keep you out of OCS, might even keep you from making corporal or tech sergeant. You're ruining what could be a great military career. I'm going to dispose of the evidence and hope for your sake the matter is never found out."

The kid looked puzzled for a moment and then relieved to learn that he was being saved from a possible firing squad. Fabian strode back down the aisle, slid into the seat next to me at the end of the car, where we shared the bottle. It was good, my favorite—Canadian Club.

Fabian Murphy had no foreboding about his future in the Army. "It is just like selling questionable securities. You don't ask them to buy, you just let them take it away from you. If I just hadn't been so busy in that boiler shop peddling paper I could have convinced the Army they needed a talented and experienced ordinance procurement officer in Manhattan where I could have spent the war scrutinizing purchase orders. Instead, one morning I receive 'Greetings from your friends and neighbors,' Some friends. I had been 'selected' as a volunteer to serve my country."

I asked him how Hope's shares of Essence of Virgin Apricot Pits turned out. "Don't know," he said. "I never did follow it. Saw it listed on the over-the-counter the day I called him. Did get a nice note from Bob the next day. Never did hear from him again."

Fabian's theory about the military in wartime was that they needed all the help they can get. "Keep in mind," he expostulated, the officers you'll be saying 'Yes, sir, No sir' to, are mostly ninety-day OCS wonders and are scared stiff, but afraid to admit it. The lowest man on the totem pole is the second lieutenant. He's blamed for everything above and below him. His superiors are going to blame him for every SNAFU they commit. There is no one he can pass it on to because every foul-up by the enlisted men is his responsibility. They strut around in their sharp uniforms but are scared silly on the inside."

"What's that got to do with us?" I said, "We're still a couple of grunts eating out of mess kits."

"It's got everything to do with us." The average soldier resents his officers. He does everything he can think of to embarrass him without involving himself. Young officers with minimum training will hand down wacky orders that can be interpreted the wrong way. You can bet that when the lower-rank non-coms, who know better, read those orders, they will be carried out the wrong way just to see how red faced their lieutenant can get.

"Now we, who like to think about what's in it for us, operate in the opposite direction. Instead of fighting the Army, we join it. We diplomatically correct garbled orders. We suggest ways to calm problems in the ranks--everything we can do to make our CO look like general staff material without—and this is important--doing anything to enhance ourselves."

I still wasn't impressed.

"What do we get out of it besides being called a brown-noser by our buddies?"

"A small price to pay," said Fabian. "Soon our officers will find they can't operate without us. They will do everything to keep us close to them. There will be subtle promotions for us with cover-up reasons: 'Particularly proefficient with disassembly of the M1 Rifle,' or 'Displays outstanding ability to maintain maximum hygienic standards in the bivouac area.' We both know the real reason: 'He saves my ass!' After promotions come special privileges. Maybe a desk, a private room in the barracks, a special place at the bar in the non-coms club, even maybe first crack at the USO girls."

"Do you really expect all this to work?"

Fabian smiled. "Watch me when we leave the train."

The train pulled on to a siding where we were greeted by an all-military young captain who informed us there would be a one-mile walk in military formation to the receiving barracks area.

"Who is in charge of this group? he barked. Fabian stepped forward smartly and acknowledged it was he. Then, before the Captain could respond, Fabian said, "Sir, one of my men, recruit Morton, has a slightly twisted ankle which might be aggravated by the walk and require hospitalization. If you would permit him to ride in the jeep it would be helpful in keeping his condition under control." The captain stared at Morton for a moment, mumbled something about goldbricks, and then ordered Morton into the jeep.

As we walked together, Fabian smiled.

"See, it's working. There is not much wrong with Morton, but our captain is worried about bringing an invalid into camp on his watch. Someone over him will say he was negligent making an injured man walk a mile, resulting in a condition requiring hospital treatment. The Captain will never admit it, but he is grateful that the matter was brought to his attention. Hope that Morton is bright enough to limp a little when he gets out of the jeep."

That night Fabian got his first perk. He was named barracks leader, which meant a private cubical for his cot.

Fabian Murphy was as sophisticated as he was confident. In his small talk there was an inoffensive air of superiority; in gatherings, listeners could detect a sympathetic tolerance for authority, and, for those who took themselves too seriously--more to be pitied than pilloried.

We were together at the reception center for only three days when, after being uniformed, immunized, and lectured on the perils of unprotective sex, we were sent in different directions. I knew then that this was a man you wanted on your side, although you didn't know why--unless you knew he could maneuver your enemies, as well as you.

I never expected to see Fabian Murphy again--but I did.

There was a major crisis aboard the FS344 when the cook reported the theft of a forty-five pound round of cheddar cheese. According to the area quartermaster, it was worth seventy-two dollars and sixty-five cents, including the special cheesecloth wrap. This was serious. Army regs required that the loss of any government property with a value greater than twenty[-five dollars be reported immediately to the senior officer of the nearest Army command. We conducted our own investigation, hoping to recover what might be left of the cheddar and avoid a reproach for lack of security over food stores while at sea. Worse, the seventy-two dollars and sixty-five cents might be deducted from my pay. Snuffy suggested we watch the individual crewmembers for signs of constipation. "Cheese is pretty binding," he said. "When we notice someone doing a lot of grunting we may have our man." This was not one of Snuffy's better ideas. How could anyone eat forty-five pounds of cheese without looking like a butter churn? And where could anyone hide enough snack crackers to make the heist palatable? No, I would have to throw myself on the mercy of the provost marshall and confess to inadequate security of government property.

We were due for the monthly regimental headquarters visit and debriefing at Camp Gordon Johnston, near Carabelle, Florida. It was a most illogical location for any kind of marine activity. There was no dockage for craft of our size and draft. The ships had to be anchored about a mile off shore; crews were lightened to a landing ramp and bused to post headquarters inland. I reported to the commandant's office and was informed that matters of missing property were being handled by the personnel officer in an adjoining office. The door was partially open, so I entered without knocking. Seated at a desk was an officer swung around to face a back table and engaged in a very detailed telephone conversation. I seemed to recall from a previous time the cut of those shoulders as he continued unconcerned about who might over hear him. "Listen, McKinstry, we've got to have the meat wagon down here by 2030 tonight. You're the Med Center supply sergeant with lots of suction, so I know you can handle it. Tell them Colonel Margin's angina pectoris is acting up again and we need an ambulance on standby tonight. We'll provide the driver and attendants. We know there's a personnel shortage--just let us have the wagon for this emergency. Mrs. Margin is deeply concerned. Don't flub it this time. The two girls are lined up and ready to fly. The Colonel's secretary, Monya, is one of them and you get first choice. I've put a lot of government time on this and you know how scarce tomatoes are on this Godforsaken post. I'll meet you at battalion headquarters, 2030. Don't be late the patients get nervous."

The speaker swung around. It was Fabian Murphy! In unison, we exclaimed, "What are you doing here?"

Fabian was delighted to see me, particularly after learning that I commanded an Army vessel. I had the uneasy feeling that already he was formulating plans which would involve the FS 344 in ways that would enhance the life of Fabian Murphy in the service of his country. His rise in rank was as rapid as my own. Where mine was a clerical mistake, his was as well planned as the invasion of a hostile country.

At Fort Sheridan in Chicago, Fabian had attached himself to a confused captain and covered the young officer's mistakes in form and protocol. He gathered for himself promotions in the enlisted ranks and then decided to shoot for a commission; he dropped subtle remarks about considering a request for a transfer. Of course, an EM cannot be granted a transfer without the approval of his commanding officer--unless it's a transfer to hazardous duty, like military
intelligence behind enemy lines, or the paratroopers, or underwater sabotage.

"Thank God they didn't call my bluff," he said. "Instead, I was appointed a warrant officer in the Transportation Corps and ended up personnel officer at this sand-and-swamp armpit of Florida."

"What's the 'meat wagon' bit you were talking about?"

Fabian laughed in that everthing-is-under-control manner of his, implying that harmless fellowship was to be encouraged if the world were to remain sane.

"It's a morale thing," he said. " 'Meat Wagon' is the camp's trade name for an ambulance, and I need one for tonight's rest and recreation. You must remember that this post is forty miles from the nearest Howard Johnson. You certainly can't schedule an assignation on a pool table in the officer's club. McKinstry owes me one. I got him his promotion to supply sergeant at the hospital. Very handy. He requisitions an ambulance for the evening. I provide the girls and cut him in on the action. We alternate the driving. An ambulance, if it's handled right, can be a pretty comfortable cubicle d'amour if the driver avoids speed bumps. Once we were pulled over by an MP patrol who wanted to know why we were driving an emergency vehicle so slowly. I explained that it was a delicate run of mercy, that we were carrying a soldier with a critical back injury, and that any sharp or sudden movement could be instantly fatal for him. I turned toward the rear and shouted to the attending 'nurse,' "How's our patient's back holding out?' She yelled, 'His back is still in one piece, but he is looking exhausted. Don't take any sharp curves.' The MP wondered why a warrant officer was driving. 'Serious personnel shortage,' I told him. 'There's no rank in an emergency.' He saluted and wished us well."

During the next few days ashore I learned about Fabian Murphy's impressive power in military matters. Camp Gordon Johnston served as a holding tank for unassigned officers. As personnel expediter, Fabian was responsible for meeting the requests for officers to fill slots for TC assignments all over the world. It was a paper-shuffling job that only Fabian could make interesting and not routine, and a window of opportunity for someone with the ability to recognize the benefits of compassionate influence—for the deliverer.

The next evening, while sharing drinks with Fabian at the makeshift officers' club, I witnessed a demonstration of his ability to control careers. Second Lt. Alder Carlton was known by all of us as an obnoxious, pseudo-aristocrat who patronized his compatriots with understanding pity for their inherited lack of couth. Off duty, he even carried a swagger stick.

Carlton came into the club while we were there and sauntered over to the bar where he carefully placed his swagger stick and ordered a "Rob Roy with an anchovy and a twist." The bartender, just off KP duty, blinked and asked the Lieutenant to repeat the order.

Carlton, with a charitable look, said, "I guess I shouldn't have expected that you had ever read Worthington's International Bartender's Guide. Just give me a beer, if you can find one with single-syllable words on the label."

Fabian turned to me and said, "Where do you want him to go?"

I thought briefly. "I know you can't send him to hell, but what about the next worst place-- Dutch Harbor in the winter?"

Two days later, I received a copy of special orders: Lt. Alder Carlson was ordered to report to the CO of a Harbor Craft Company at Dutch Harbor in the Aleutians, with possible transfer to Adak as soon as that island was secured by American forces. I hope he took his swagger stick.

My initial problem, the Cheddar Cheese Caper, had yet to be handled. It was routine for Fabian. He assigned one of the waiting shave-tails to be investigating officer. He pointed out that the young officer, hoping never to be assigned duty in the field, would drag the investigation on for so long that the matter would become mired in paper and eventually be sidetracked to the Pentagon and lost forever.

After reuniting with Fabian, I began to get unusual sailing orders. One called for the FS344 to transport the post band to St Petersburg for the purpose of entertaining a small cantonment of soldiers over a three-day weekend. Reason was that this contingent of twenty-two men had been neglected and denied the usual recreation facilities of the main post. In actuality, these guys were having a ball, on their own with minimum duty in the Tampa-Saint Pete area where there were plenty of girls and bars. I could smell the Irish touch of a Fabian Murphy. Of course, the thirty-one band members could not be trusted away from post on their own. There would have to be a responsible officer in charge. Guess who. W.O. Fabian Murphy.

We arrived at the Saint Pete Coast Guard dock on a Friday morning, and didn't see Fabian again until the time of sailing on Monday morning. He came aboard looking haggard but contented. The trip back across the Gulf was uncomfortable, hot and sultry, with conditions below deck unbearable. Naval regulations forbade smoking or lights of any kind on deck at night—might attract enemy aircraft. Our passengers were not happy campers.

Fabian, as morale officer, had a solution. Bring the bandsmen on deck, set up their stands, and let them play swing music the rest of the night and keep everyone entertained. One hitch. The band said they needed illumination to read the music. No problem for Fabian. Turn on the two bridge floodlights and direct them down to the deck. At this point I protested: we would be breaking Naval regulations. There could be no lights on deck.

Fabian very gently took me aside and softly explained the gravity of the situation. "We are overcrowded and the men are enduring almost steerage conditions," he said. "We might have a mutiny on our hands, and how would that look on your records?"

"Might be better than being brought before a Naval board of inquiry and ending up a mess sergeant on the Eastern Front."

"Nothing to worry about," Fabian assured me. "Nobody out here to see us. You and I know there are no enemy planes flying over the Gulf of Mexico. Here's a chance to be respected by our men. Let's not muff it."

"Okay," I said, "But sign a statement assuming all responsibility. You take the heat—otherwise, no lights on my ship."

Fabian smiled. "You got it," he said. "Bring on your statement. I thrive on rightful responsibility."

Snuffy prepared an official-looking missive that made Fabian responsible for everything from illegal lighting aboard ship to the lack of bar soap in the showers. He signed without reading it, or even asking for a copy.

Everything went well, we thought. The bandsmen moved up on deck, set up their stands, and the ship rocked with swing the rest of the night. It did get everyone's mind off the oppressive heat. The cook brought coffee and cookies. Someone, probably Fabian, didn't think it festive enough. Mysteriously all the other lights of the ship came on, running lights, anchor lights, signal lights, until we looked like a floating Christmas tree, a moonlight excursion boat under full sail.

But we weren't alone. On a reciprocal course, our sister ship, the FS343, was heading south. Later, as Captain Charlie Harper described the sight: "We thought it was a Grant Park New Year's Eve celebration coming toward us, with an ear-spitting rendition of 'Hold That Tiger!' We tried to signal but the volume of the music and the Broadway illumination obscured our horn and blinker lamp." When Harper reached Tampa the next morning, he filed an official report of his unusual midnight sighting.

Our reception back at headquarters was not encouraging. I was served with a notice to appear before a board of inquiry to determine whether a court-martial was in order. I dug out Fabian's signed statement and told him I planned to dump the entire matter on him.

"Forget the statement," he said. "It won't hold up. As master of the ship, you are fully responsible for not only the vessel but for the actions of everyone aboard. Under no circumstances can you pass on your responsibility."

"You mean you're going to let me hang," I shouted, "after you put the whole thing together?"

Fabian was as cool as ever. "Have I ever let you down? Remember the Cheese Caper, when you thought you were going to pay for a seventy-five dollar round of cheddar? I'll be with you at the inquiry. Before you have a chance to be questioned, I'll butt in and take responsibility for the whole thing."

"Do you mean to take the rap, then?"

"Of course not," he said, "but I may make heroes out of both of us. Just don't flash that damn statement you made me sign. That could hang you from the yardarm."

True to his promise, Fabian appeared at the inquiry looking as unconcerned as a jaywalker about to explain why he ignored a red light. Before I could be questioned, Fabian stepped forward, apologized to the board, and asked permission to explain his position on the ship that night. He pointed to me and wished to go on record commending me for the action I had taken on that fateful night, "a decision that probably saved seventy-four lives, and possibly many more."

The attention of the court swung from me to this authoritative figure, ready to reveal the true story. Officer Fabian Murphy smiled and began: "It was with grateful relief that I observed the spilt-second action of this ship master in avoiding an almost certain collision at sea. At approximately 0130, the lookout on duty discerned and reported the outline of a fully-load, blacked-out transport about to overrun us. Head on, close-to-gale-force winds kept the sound of our horn from reaching the transport. There was no change in its collision course with the FS344. Most of us felt that disaster was inevitable, until this ship commander made the decision to switch on every available lighting piece aboard. The sudden burst of illumination alerted the transport which immediately changed course, narrowly averting a collision. It is with relief and gratitude that we of the FS344 thank our skipper for saving our lives."

There was a moment of silence until one of the board members cleared his throat and said, "What about the report of band music coming from the ship?"

Fabian smiled. "Thank you, sir, for using the word 'music.' I was the officer in charge of the band we were bringing back from entertaining troops at St Petersburg. I take pride in the beautiful music they produce. However, on the night of the near-collision, it was just noise. The band was on deck cooling off. When it was detected that our signals were not being heard, they contributed what they could by sounding their instruments at full volume, in the most raucous tones they could muster. It was not music, but thank you for saying so."

I was spellbound. I understood now why Fabian Murphy was able to peddle all those questionable securities even to Bob Hope.

The inquiry was dissolved with no further action. Fabian said there was always the chance I might get a medal. I asked him about the transport bit. He said there was an African-bound transport out of New Orleans that night, but its course was one-hundred fifty miles west of ours. "You must recognize," he said, "that the six members of the inquiry board have never been in a boat. The closest they ever get to water is in a shower stall. We could have told them the bilge water was on fire and we were signaling for help."

Two weeks later while at sea, I received a communication from Fabian: "You are being ordered through the Panama Canal for a training rendezvous in the Pacific. Should be a three-week ball before you return. Maybe I can wangle a temporary assignment with you. Never been through the Canal. Panama is famous for hats—and girls."

None of the crew had been through the Canal so we looked forward with some eagerness to the experience of crossing a mountain range without hiring mules. Knowing that our ship-handling expertise did not quite match that of Admiral Halsey's, and having heard stories of inept skippers running their crafts aground and blocking the gaillard cut for weeks and finishing their tour of duty as parking-lot attendants for tugboats in New Guinea, I was justifiably nervous.

Adding to my apprehension was word from Fabian Murphy that he had maneuvered a three-week temporary duty assignment aboard the FS344 as "morale officer." This was a period that would take Fabian through the Canal with us and return him to his home base in time to resume his wheeling-dealing at Regimental Headquarters without missing a beat. As personnel officer, he had created a nest of influence that made his military life very comfortable. For the rest of the war, Fabian intended to enjoy the benefits provided by those who discovered they "owed him one." He welcomed this government-provided cruise through the Canal as an appropriate environment for celebrating his recent promotion to first lieutenant. I had hoped for an experienced marine officer to help keep us out of shoal water. Instead, I got a "morale officer."

The voyage to Colon was not exactly a carnival cruise. Fabian had difficulty finding his sea legs and was seasick most of the trip. Orders came sending the ship to Mobile, Alabama, to pick up provisions—fourteen cases of food to feed the crew until we reached the Canal Zone. At the Mobile quartermaster pier, the assigned space was not much greater than the length of the ship. It would take some skilled maneuvering (which we seemed short of) to get alongside without wiping out a section of the dock and the neatly stacked eases of food that awaited us. Two small Navy tankers lay next to each other directly ahead of our allotted pier space. It was Thanksgiving Day and the officers of the tankers had gathered in the wardroom of the inboard vessel, some with their visiting families, for a holiday dinner and to give thanks for being in Alabama and not Guadalcanal. Little did they know that potential disaster lay just a few yards abaft their stern in the form of a friendly but formidable, out-of-control Army freighter, the FS344.

Ships are normally controlled by a "telegraph" signal system for each engine. The officer on the bridge "rings" an order to the engine room for slow, half or full, ahead or back, as well as stop and "finished with engines." When a signal is received by the chief engineer, he repeats the order by "ringing" back on the telegraph an acknowledgement of the order to prevent any misunderstanding.

The FS344 was a state-of-the-art (1940) vessel with a pair of high-speed twin-screw GM diesel engines and, most advanced, if not very dependable, a supplementary electronic system that allowed the bridge officer to control directly the pair of engines waiting for directions below. By-passing the antiquated telegraph system was a heady experience for a young officer who still had trouble distinguishing the bow from the stern. A dual set of controls at each end of the bridge enabled the conning officer to handle the ship like a picnic launch at a boat club regatta – provided those mysterious switches, fuses, conductors, and other unpronounceable technological advances were not beyond their ninety-day warranties.

Everything seemed to be going well as I eased the bow to within several yards of the tanker's stern on this quiet holiday afternoon. It was an ideal time to demonstrate our direct control system of modern ship handling. We were moving slowly ahead and it was time to stop. I pulled back both control handles to "slow astern" and waited for the response. There was none. Instead, we continued to move forward. It must be the tide and current propelling us. The sterns of the two ships were looming close. Frantically, I pulled the controls to "full astern." The response was immediate: the ship leaped forward at full speed toward the moored tankers. The speaking tube from the engine room came to life. It was the chief engineer. "The directional solenoid switch has blown! You're stuck in full ahead!" It was a time for prayer. But Snuffy, who was at the wheel, had a better idea. Without orders from anyone, he swung the bow so that we struck the stern breast line, snapping it like a shoelace, and drove our ship between the tightly lashed-together tankers. We severed their mooring lines, except for the bowline. Finally, we stopped, wedged tightly between the two vessels. The force of our drive smashed their porthole wind scoops flat against the hull, cutting off all daylight from the below-deck quarters. It sounded like a single explosive demolishing a three-storied building. The diners aboard the inboard tanker thought it was a second Pearl Harbor. The wardroom plunged into darkness as the portholes welded shut. When the diners poured out on deck, they were astonished to find an Army freighter now parked affectionately between them and the outboard tanker. It was an embarrassing moment for me as I stood on the wing of the bridge to survey the results of an unplanned naval engagement. It took three hours and the efforts of all crews to move the FS344 back to its assigned berth. Later, I went aboard the first tanker to extend my regrets to the skipper and to find out when the Department of the Navy would nail me to the wall.

    I was pleasantly surprised to find I was dealing with a compassionate and understanding young Navy commander. I tried to explain the technical glitches that had caused the alteration with his ship, but he interrupted me with, "Don't worry about it. We all make mistakes. It happened to me in New York harbor where I took the end off a Staten Island ferryboat. I had everything going for me, too. Commander of a destroyer, in line for flotilla duty overseas, when I took time off to visit the head. The wrong time. Really wasn't my fault. The court said it was my responsibility, and now my command is this crummy little tanker that has trouble getting out of the harbor without help."

    Each time I tried to tell him about solenoid switches, he cut me off and told me to forget the incident. Miraculously, the only damage, other than my pride, was the smashed windscoops and a missing taftrail flagstaff from the outboard tanker. "I won't even log it," he said. "There will be no investigation and there will be nothing to keep you from going overseas and being blown out of the water."

Problems didn't stop. There were fourteen stacks of cased food on the pier. We were told to load fourteen cases and move on to the Canal Zone. Crewmen Aristotle and Leondro were on duty, and, forgetting past experiences with these two Greek Lotharios, I assigned them the task of going ashore and moving the fourteen food cases to the ship. They completed the job promptly and we moved out to sea.

That night the puzzled cook came to me and reported that he had opened all the food cases and discovered we had fourteen cases of nothing but grapefruit!

Then it hit me: Aristotle and Leondro had forgotten instructions and had taken fourteen cases from the same stock. This meant that some other ship would probably have two cases of prime-rib steaks. Facing the FS344 was five days of nothing but grapefruit! It was time for our morale officer, Fabian Murphy, to find a solution.

He thought a moment and said, "Between here and Panama there are shrimp and oyster boats all over the place. When we spot one, we sail over and imply we've a government inspection team looking for saboteurs. As we approach them, we keep that fake foredeck gun trained on them as if we mean business. We tell them how important citrus is to a fisherman's diet and suggest that they trade some oysters and shrimp for a case of fresh grapefruit. They'll be so happy they passed the inspection, they will probably want to trade some of that awful rum they carry aboard. Don't take it though -- tastes like varnish."

"How do we find that many shrimp boats?" I said.

"No problem," said Fabian. "We put the crew on alert for submarines. Post them in the crow's nest and every other high spot with binoculars. Order them to report every object they see. Anything that looks like a fishing boat, we investigate."

It worked. We had shrimp and oysters with an occasional grapefruit for five days. Fabian warned me to restrict the crew to the ship in the Canal Zone. "You know those Latins, and you know what an oyster diet does for the male libido."

As we approached Colon and anchored in place for our turn to enter Gatun Locks, I became apprehensive and wondered if it wouldn't have been more prudent for the Army to have sent us around Cape Horn, three-thousand more miles but less hazardous for ships inclined to run into things. Finally, we received the signal to approach the first lock. Everything seemed to be going well as we passed the channel markers on the proper side and there were no angry communications from shore stations.

We could see the opened locks gates ahead, and, on instructions, slowed our speed to crawl. Then it happened.

The steersman said, with a helpless look: "It won't respond. We're swinging to port!"

Horrified, I saw that we were turning broadside in the channel. Once again, the state-of-the-art electronic gear had struck. The solenoid gizmo had blown and we were going to enter sideways! The tide was carrying us into the locks and I had visions of jamming up the Canal for the rest of the war. Canal personnel had the same thoughts. Three small tugs raced out from the shore station in a frantic effort to unscramble the situation. The current was carrying us closer to the gates and by the time the tugs had straightened the ship we were entering the locks – but stern first! We couldn't swing the bow in proper direction, but we did avoid damage to the lock. Once in it, the side-mounted electric mules got their lines on the ship and began towing us through. We were probably the first ship ever to go through the Panama Canal backwards. A dubious honor.

Army ordnance came aboard. By the time we reached the Miraflores lock, our steering system was back in operation, but without factory warranty. The lockmaster suggested if we ever returned, that we might try Cape Horn.

We were ordered to proceed to San Diego for one week of training maneuvers with several other ships to learn how not to run into each other. Fabian was getting bored and eager to get back to regimental headquarters to resume his position of unofficial influence. His three-week temporary assignment aboard ship had convinced him God never intended that he should be a sailor. Also, a good martini with dinner at the officers' club was far more satisfying than the hash we served on the FS344.

Something was going on that made me uncomfortable. For the first time, the Army became concerned about our inoperative forty-mm gun on the bow. An ordnance crew came out to the anchorage, raised the barrel from the hold, positioned it on the mount, and pronounced it "ready for action."

Several cases of fifty-caliber ammunition for the two bridge-mounted machine guns arrived on board. Personnel people visited us to review individual records of each crew member and to make certain that everyone had a will. We had never received this much attention before. It was both flattering and discomforting. Fabian Murphy said it was his presence that did it, that G3 was afraid he might write an unfavorable report of our fitness status. We both hoped he was right.

How to Stay Afloat Wearing Army Boots

Chapter Ten

Our exercise in ship handling and learning how to avoid running into other vessels in close quarters was a disappointment. We came within inches of sinking a minesweeper when Lt. Baldwin became confused and couldn't remember whether two blasts of the whistle meant "I'm holding to starboard." Or was it port? In charge of the maneuvers was a gloomy Colonel Blimp type Navy captain who continuously lamented his ill fortune in being assigned the responsibility of making a ragtag fleet of questionable craft seaworthy and ready to take on whatever the Japanese Imperial Fleet had to offer. On one occasion, he asked what agricultural college had prepared me for sea duty. Captain Roger Drumond was a World War One retread. Safely retired after 20 years of Naval service aboard a destroyer, he had been recalled to serve as a co-ordinating officer between the Army and Navy in an effort to get both services to speak the same nautical language. Not an easy assignment, considering that the Army called anything that floated, regardless of size, a "boat."

The crew seemed to be enjoying the operation, albeit with some embarrassment when other sailors ribbed them about being dragged through the Canal stern first. The exception was Fabian who was becoming bored with a limited audience (just a crew of eighteen) to practice his charm on. He did manage to sell a life-insurance policy to Elwood Corbin, our not-so-bright lookout. The benefits were unusual and generous: if the ship, with Elwood aboard, sank anywhere west of the International Date Line, and under a full moon, triple indemnity would be paid and Elwood's mother would be independent for the rest of her life. Elwood was grateful for the opportunity to share in this limited offer available only to look-outs and full-time coal-stokers aboard military vessels. The one person not captivate by the fabulous Fabian Murphy was Montgomery Morgan, scion of American Revolutionaries and protector of life styles on Martha's Vineyard. Whenever Fabian's name was mentioned, Monty would sniff through his hawk-like nose and mutter something about "second-generation Irish, worse than Sicilian Mafia. "Fabian knew that Monty's fortune was controlled under a rigid trust that would allow no wiggle room for a well-meaning con man like Lt. Murphy. His gifts of persuasion would be wasted, so he resorted to a malapropian response that left Monty confused, not knowing whether to pity this lace-curtain Irishman or ostracize him totally from cultural congeniality. Over coffee in the wardroom one morning Fabian, in all innocence, asked Monty if there were any Jews in his long line of blueblood forbears, or were all his ancestors *genitals*? For one moment Monty was aghast. His government-issued wire-rim spectacles slid down the point of his hawk nose before he could reply. Deciding that this was another display of Irish ignorance, he responded in a condescending tone.

"Our lineage goes back to the Mayflower, originally Puritans. We're proud to say that Cotton Mather was one of our more noted ancestors."

Fabian brightened and pressed on. "Oh, yeah, Cotton Mather; he was a real conservative, wasn't he? Or was he one of those left genitals? Some of those right genitals have been a pain in the ass."

Red-faced, Montgomery Morgan rose to his feet and with a snort left the room, muttering something about shanty Irish mental limitations. Fabian shouted a quick apology, saying that he hoped his remarks had not "embezzled" Lt. Morgan in any way.

Our training assignment, maneuvering with other ships off the California coast, had been extended from the original three weeks to four. This distressed Fabian Murphy. He feared that his temporary duty was beginning to backfire and that some eager, power-hungry officer at post headquarters might be usurping his realm of unauthorized influence. He tried to convince Calfornia command headquarters that his presence back at camp Gordon Johnston was essential, and that he should be flown there immediately. Response to his request was a firm negative with the suggestion that he file an appeal with the Department of Defense and hope the war wasn't over before it was processed.

We were finally told that the training period was over and to stand by for further orders. Fabian informed his San Diego lady friends that all good things must end, but to keep in touch for the time when he might take up residence at Lajolla with other retired admirals.

The next morning I was awakened at four-fifteen by the communications officer with a message from Captain Drumond ordering the ship to be ready to sail within the hour, no later that 0530. One hour later, a second message came ordering us to weigh anchor, take our position with the fleet, and be prepared for an extended voyage. This was it. We knew now that we were on our way across the Pacific. The question was, would the ragtag fleet ever make it? In addition to the FS344, there were two wooden mine-sweepers, a one-hundred seventy-five foot Tuna boat, a 1923 Great Lake whale-back freighter, which from fifty yards appeared to be a submarine, a coastal coal-burning packet ship from Panama, an impressive diesel-powered three-masted schooner upon which it was said Douglas Fairbanks entertained Mary

Pickford on their honeymoon, and finally a World War One destroyer commanded by the fleet Captain, Roger Drumond. Captain Drumond was always gloomy, expressing doubt that he would ever get this motley group of jetsam much beyond the harbor, let alone the South Pacific. He was comforted by the doubt that a Japanese U-Boat captain would ever waste a torpedo on any of us. Deep in his thoughts was that someone in the Naval Department was repaying him for a poker bet he welched on during World War One.

Around 0600 Fabian Murphy, still in his skivvies, burst onto the bridge, wild-eyed and shouting. In the excitement of going to sea no one had thought about waking him; besides, as an executive-type officer, Fabian had always said he did his best thinking in the morning and should not be disturbed before 0900.

In an unfamiliar voice he shrieked, "What's happening! Where are we going? How do I get ashore? I don't belong to you guys, I belong to the Army Southern Command!"

At the wheel, Snuffy softly murmured, "Today, we all belong to God."

"Oh, shut up!" said Fabian. "I demand to be put ashore. Where's the launch? I'll take that."

While he was catching his breath, I explained that we were probably on our way to Okinawa, and that I realized he was only temporarily assigned to the ship and not part of the regular complement. I told him I would communicate with Captain Drumond, Convoy Commander, and ask him to address the problem.

"He better damn well take care of it," threatened Fabian. "When post headquarters hears that I've been literally kidnapped there will be hell to pay!"

I got word to Captain Drumond that I had an unassigned temporary duty officer aboard who because of his essential duties state-side required immediate transfer to his post in Florida. I could almost hear Captain Drumond sigh when I read his response: "I knew that if you and your ship got out of the harbor without running aground there would be some other goof-up. I will get a signal to the Transportation Command and find out what they want done."

When I showed the message to Fabian, he became his usual confident self. "When Corps discovers I'm out here with a bunch of retarded swabbies, I'll be ashore before the next watch. They may have to send out a fast cutter to take me off, but staff knows I'm needed at headquarters."

Three hours later, Drumond beamed a message: No need to be concerned. War Department says orders are being cut transferring Lt. Murphy to permanent duty aboard the FS344. Problem solved. Now Fabian was one of us. When I showed the message to him he stared in disbelief, then began to scream. "It's a forgery! That Drumond is trying to be a comedian! Throw the launch over or I'll drive myself ashore."

When he stopped for breath I told him to cool it. "We're twenty miles from shore. The launch doesn't have that much diesel aboard. Besides that, we have our orders to follow. You're under my command now and my first order to you is to simmer down and start learning how to distinguish the bow from the stern."

For the first time, Fabian was without words. In a low, hoarse voice, he said, "Where is the chief engineer's cabin?" He knew that Lt. Ronald Cuthburt had a secret cache of Bourbon he was always ready to share with a fellow traveler.

It would be eighteen months before Lt. Fabian Murphy would again see any part of the continental United States.

Chapter Eleven

The advantage of a convoy is its difficulty to get lost. Out of our eight mismatched vessels, one was certain to know the way. Thanks to Lt. Baldwin, the FS344 got lost the second night out. Baldwin was a philatelist who felt that stamps were made to be pasted in books and drooled over with fellow collectors on long winter nights, never to be sullied by being stuck on an unsanitary envelope and dropped into an unappreciative mailbox. Passing through the Canal Zone, he acquired an uncancelled sheet of Nicaraguan Correos featuring the likeness of Franklin Roosevelt. Before he could catalog this newest addition to his collection, he discovered that Fabian Murphy had taken three of them to use on a letter he was sending to a lady in Chicago whom he had promised to marry when the war was over. Fabian couldn't understand Baldwin's hysteria when he found the violated sheet of intaglio-printed commemoratives. "There was no real theft," Fabian said. "I left three dollars and sixty cents to cover the face value of the stamps, and that was fifteen cents too much, but I didn't have the exact change."

Baldwin was not to be appeased. He told me, "I demand that Fabian be charged with grand larceny and conduct unbecoming an officer! He should be reduced in rank and sent to Leavenworth for an indeterminate term!"

It was a tense moment until Fabian took his accuser aside. "See here, Baldwin, you are due for a leave in two months."

"With my influence at headquarters your leave could be extended an additional ten days. And I'll instruct my Chicago girlfriend to return the envelope with the cancelled correos."

"What of the reduced value because of the cancellation marks?"

Fabian reluctantly said not to be concerned.

"I will allow you to buy my share of a Peruvian gold mine stock I've been saving for my elderly uncle now confined to a rest home near Temperance, Michigan."

Fabian had a copy of a letter written by the president of the Peruvian Republic which stated that within 90 days these gilt-edged securities would triple in value, an investment opportunity usually reserved for mothers and very close friends. It was an offer Baldwin could not resist. He forgave his transgressor and visualized the number of uncirculated, first-issue sheets of stamps he could purchase with his profits. Of course, there was no way Fabian could have known that Peru was in the middle of a revolution that overturned the government and nationalized all natural resources. He did know that we were headed overseas and that all leaves for personnel outside the continental US had been cancelled for the duration. It was Lt. Baldwin's obsession with stamps that brought the FS344 close to becoming the lost flying Dutchman of the Pacific.

Navy Captain Roger Drumond was not a happy sailor. As a retread from the first World War, he expected his duties this time around to be dramatic enough to command the attention of the Depart of the Navy and possibly lead to a promotion to rear admiral. It didn't happen that way. Instead, his assignment was to lead a flotilla of eight misbegotten watercraft into the South Pacific.

Worse, all the ships, including his own destroyer, were crewed by Army personnel—a sort of ecumenical demonstration of inter-service equality.

The evening before departing San Diego harbor, Captain Drumond was having his final bourbon at the Naval officer's club while lamenting his fate at the hands of the gods of war who had seen fit to put him in command of an obsolete destroyer named the "Millard Fillmore." It was a final humiliation. "Of our presidents, I end up with a ship named after the most do-nothing one of all!" he said. "If this isn't demeaning enough, I have been assigned to lead eight mismatched, barely-afloat excursion boats across the Pacific. That may be the easy part. The real service-above-self is that I've been ordered to turn these Army grunts into the equivalent of US Navy sailors! Have you ever tried to turn a mule into a derby-winning thoroughbred? See what I mean? It's enough to make a career man consider going over the hill."

It was 0500 when the convoy left its anchorage and already bets were being laid on who would be the first to ram another ship. I was pleased to learn that odds on the FS344 were less than twenty-percent—an indicator that we were learning from past mistakes. The first day was uneventful. Elwood Corbin, lookout first class, kept announcing every five minutes that the Tiapa, the Panamanian riverboat, was directly ahead off our starboard bow. Elwood had a strong voice, and, after three hours of continual announcements, it was time to have a talk with him. Fabian took on the assignment. He explained that the Tiapa had been assigned that position in the convoy and would probably be there, just off our bow, for the rest of the trip across the Pacific and it was not necessary to keep telling us every five minutes. Elwood was offended and protested: "The Modern Seamanship Manual says the lookout must report everything he sees, and I see the Tiapa."

Patiently, Fabian agreed but explained that this was a delicate reverse situation that required all the talents of a skilled lookout. "We are entering a war zone, which means it is also essential for you to report what you don't see." Elwood looked puzzled. Fabian continued, "Whenever you look ahead and don't see the Tiapa, then report it. Sound the alarm. It will be mentioned in the log book, with your name, stating that you were the first person to alert the captain that something wasn't there." Elwood looked pleased and went back to reporting whales and dolphins.

The second day was different. We got lost. It was apparent that Captain Drumond, on occasion, was vicariously living in a World War One past where he commanded a destroyer in the Atlantic. He seemed to have acquired a submarine phobia that still haunted him. In a meeting with the eight skippers of his fleet, he warned us we could expect harassment from the unseen enemy at anytime during our voyage to the South Pacific. It was scary to hear him relate the havoc wreaked by the German undersea wolf pack during the North Atlantic struggle to supply the European allies. It was a disappointment to the middle-aged warrior of the deep that we never saw or detected a single submarine.

During the morning watch of the second day out, Captain Drumond alerted us that he suspected we were being shadowed by an enemy sub. If signs of danger indicated possible attack, the fleet would be ordered to break formation temporarily and disperse briefly on separate courses to reduce the size of a target made up of eight ships grouped together. Each of us would sail on a separate heading for a limited time before being recalled back to formation. The assumption was that no U-boat captain would want to risk disclosing his position just to knock off a lone non-descript ship of our size. If we were in convoy formation, it might be tempting to waste a couple of torpedoes, and, for target practice, wipeout all eight of the valiant little ships.

During the first hour of his watch, Lt. Baldwin was in the chart room working on his stamp collection, classifying and separating the rare from the mundane with the passion of a high-schooler trying to decide which girl to ask to the prom. Just as he discovered he had four uncancelled 1944 Polish Monte Casinos, the signalman interrupted his excitement with a message from Capt. Drumond:

"Change course to two-eight-three. Hold for fifteen minutes and await orders to regroup." Annoyed by this rupture of his concentration, Baldwin shoved the message on to his stack of commemoratives, left the chartroom and ordered the wheelman to put the ship on course two-eight-three for fifty minutes, then returned to his cataloging.

At 0800 I climbed to the bridge to relieve Baldwin. Looking through a light haze, I felt there was something wrong. Then it hit me – where was everybody? We were all alone on a vast sea of nothing. I grabbed Baldwin.

"Where have you taken us? Where's the convoy?"

"Don't sweat it," said the dapper Lieutenant. "Just following orders. Changed course to two-eight-three for fifty minutes at 0415."

He shoved the crumpled message in my hand and added, "Believe it or not, I think I've found an imperfect airmail in my collection—may be worth a bundle."

I looked at Drumond's message. "You turkey! This says to hold course for fifteen minutes, not fifty!"

Baldwin looked again.

"You're right, Skipper. You've got to talk to that signalman. He can write clearer than that."

Montgomery Morgan joined us, trailed by Fabian and engineer Lt. Ronald Cuthburt. As navigation officer, Monty did some quick calculating. "We're about thirty-five miles from our last position. Can't use the radio cause it's verboten in wartime at sea. Drumond probably tried to reach us by blinker. Probably thinks we've been knocked off by one of his imaginary subs and hopes he's right. I won't know where we are until sundown when we can shoot some stars."

It was a lonely feeling. We had never been this far from shore before, one of Captain Drumond's ducklings who had strayed. "Maybe we can just pack it in and head for home." Fabian said.

"Not a chance," I said." If someone doesn't find us soon we will be declared AWOL and put on the Army's hit list. One of your rivals at headquarters will spread the word we've sold out to the enemy."

Then third-mate Barry Darrow suggested a practical idea.

"There must be flares in the life rafts. We could fire them and the Fillmore might see them and track us down."

It worked. Three hours later, we spotted the trusty Fillmore steaming over the horizon, looking for Drumond's burden. For the moment, we were jubilant. Then we realized that someone was going to have to rationalize all this. For the first time, the officers were unanimous. As Captain and authoritative figure, I would explain to Captain Drumond the very logical circumstances that caused the FS344 to become lost. For a moment I wished we had never been found.

The Fillmore stood off while its launch with Captain Drumond aboard came alongside.

Lt. Darrow whispered, "This is the end for Baldwin. Drumond will use him for target purposes."

"I heard that," a pale Lt. Baldwin protested. "It wasn't my fault that the damn signalman can't write straight!"

Fabian offered to help. "I'll defend you for twenty-percent of your stamp collections," he said. "But I select the twenty-percent."

A red-faced Drumond was now climbing over the scuppers on the port well-deck, briefly tripping over a cleat as he tried to salute the aft ensign. His middle-age girth was not helping matters. I tried to think of an appropriate military greeting for the occasion but all that came out was, "Welcome aboard, sir. You are just in time for lunch."

Captain Drumond stared at me and through clenched teeth growled, "Stow it. I wouldn't trust this ship to serve me a cup of coffee! Do you realize you have held up the convoy for over twenty-four hours and cost your government thousands of dollars? Now, I want a complete explanation – and don't expect me to believe it."

At that moment a voice from the bow boomed, "The Tiapa is not off the starboard bow!" The Captain stopped in mid sentence. "What in the hell is that?"

"That's Corporal Elwood Corbin, our lookout," Monty Morgan said "He's is reporting what isn't there."

The Captain gaped at Monty. "He reports what he doesn't see?"

Fabian stepped forward briskly. "Sir, it's a matter of combining ship safety with morale building. Corporal Corbin feels obligated to report everything he sees. He sees the Tiapa in continuous convoy formation and so he reports continuously.

The off-watch crew complained that these minute-by-minute announcements were keeping them awake. So we solved the problem by instructing Elwood to report only if the Tiapa was missing. Because we are off course right now, the Tiapa isn't there, so Elwood is calling our attention to the missing ship. When the Fillmore leaves us to return to the convoy, our lookout will tell us the Fillmore is gone."

Captain looked at him as if examining a three-headed sturgeon. "You mean that if your lookout sees me standing here, he will say nothing? But when I leave he will report that I am missing?"

"That's sort of about it, sir," said Fabian.

The Captain doubled his chin. "I want to meet the star idiot who was the watch officer when my message was received."

Not wanting to up-stage anyone, we all stood back leaving Lt. Baldwin center stage. He was pale and sweating as he awaited the inevitable inquisition. Drumond stared at him with contempt and finally barked, "Okay, Mister. Spill it."

Baldwin cleared his throat and in a strained falsetto began detailing the events that led the FS344 to end up forty-five miles off course.

"Where were you when you received my orders?" said Drumond.

"In the chartroom stowing away my stamps," said Baldwin.

The Captain raised an eyebrow. "Stamps? What stamps? Expect to do some heavy correspondence, Lieutenant? Don't you know overseas military personnel have franking privileges for their letters? You don't need postage."

"No, no," said Baldwin. "This was my stamp collection, valuable stamps."

Captain Drumond smiled. "Don't you know, son, that the value of stamps is their face value? Collecting is a nice hobby, but only the philatelist who recognizes rare stamps can acquire a collection worth the time and effort. Have fun with your collecting but don't bet the farm on it. I know what I'm talking about because I am a philatelist." He leaned back to catch the expression on Baldwin's face.

"But I'm a philatelist, too," said Baldwin. "I even know that the word is Greek and means *love and free of tax*."

"You, a philatelist?" said Drumond. "What makes you think you are? Do you have any rare stamps or imperfects?"

"I've got a Deutches Reich overprinted German from World War One, and a five-cent Franklin, 1892. Got a planographic overprint French Air-Mail, too."

Captain Drumond's mouth dropped open. "You've got a five-cent 1892 Franklin? I have to see that. I own a Cape of Good Hope Triangle. Maybe we can trade."

Excitement was building. Baldwin took the Captain to his cabin where the two philatelists poured over the second mate's collection of commemoratives, cancellations, intaglios, and imperfects. The rest of us stood by on the deck and tried to keep Elwood from reporting that the Captain was missing.

When they returned, we heard the Captain confess in quiet tones that his upside-down center, twenty-four-cent Air Mail was actually a counterfeit that he kept in his collection to impress uninformed visitors.

As Drumond was boarding the launch, he turned to Baldwin and said, "Climb aboard, Rockford. I want to show you my collection on the Fillmore. You'll eat your heart out over a couple of first-issues British Guineas."

And so we followed the Fillmore back to the convoy where we took our position astern of the Tiapa. Our trespasses had been forgiven.

How to Stay Afloat Wearing Army Boots

Chapter Twelve

Crossing the Pacific was not exactly the blue-water cruise we had anticipated. By comparison, the Gulf of Mexico and the Atlantic coast were like lily ponds in Central Park. At 0530 on the third morning out, a flag signal from the Fillmore alerted us to expect some "inclemency" for the next seventy-two hours. Almost immediately swells grew heavier. The bow wavered from side to side as the storm's fury began to build. Steering response was like a sullen child to the helmsman's directions.

Most alarming was the pitch and roll. The inclinometer showed one pitch at forty-four degrees, bringing the propellers out of the water. Rolls were as great as forty-seven degrees, putting footprints on the bulkhead walls as we tried to get from one space to another. The cook had neglected to secure his utensils. Trays, plates, and cups were flying all over the gallery. Water slushed through the compartments. Classified publications and codebooks floated across the decks. Lt. Baldwin began to scream, "My stamps! How will we save my stamps!" The only response was from Snuffy, who shouted over the fury of the storm, " It's women and children first, then your stamps!" Lt. Monty Morgan was the only person who seemed to welcome the potential disaster that was threatening us.

"Ever since the American Revolution," he intoned, "each generation of Morgans has provided a defender of his country. Now it is my turn. There will be a plaque in the Morgan compound at Martha's Vineyard. It will say that Lt. Montgomery Morgan remained at his post to the end and went down with his ship."

At that moment Chief Engineer Cuthburt bounded up the ladder and shouted, "Stow the eulogy, Monty! We've got a fire in the aft generator and need help! Get down there and show the crew how a blueblood handles an emergency! You can drown yourself after the fire's out!"

By the time Monty reached the generator area, the fire was under control, but he added a notation about "volunteering for hazardous duty at a time of peril" to his military resume.

For the following three days peanut butter and cheese sandwiches became the menu. We began putting things back together, but the swells continued and the FS344 behaved like a hobbyhorse with the stern trying to overtake the bow vertically. Of course, there was *mal de mer*. During the worst of the storm, we had thoughts only of survival. Now seasickness was among us.

It was third mate Barry Darrow who first reported to me that Snuffy was selling a seasickness cure to afflicted sailors at a price of six dollars for a three-ounce bottle. According to Darrow, who enjoyed reporting infractions, the elixir in some cases proved to be helpful. It did not stop the nausea but the affected victim seemed to tolerate the discomfort with less complaint—and in some instances appeared to enjoy it.

Of course, dispensing unauthorized medicines was a serious matter and had to be investigated. I called upon Lt. Fabian Murphy to assist me. By paying a markup to one of the crewmen, Fabian acquired a bottle of Snuffy's cure-all and we decided to conduct a controlled analysis of the contents in the privacy of my cabin. Fabian pulled the cork, sniffed the aroma like a Parisian sommelier, and downed the full three ounces in one gulp. For a moment he stared into space, then smacked his lips and pronounced it, "Not bad, not bad at all. I've had worse at the bar in the Palmer Pump Room."

"What's that sweet smell?" I said. "It smells like my Aunt's Christmas cookies."

Fabian pursed his lips. "Vanilla!" he shouted. "This is pure vanilla extract which is ninety-percent alcohol. No wonder everybody is so happy."

"It's time to talk to Snuffy," I said. "Call him in."

I was usually uncomfortable interviewing Snuffy. There was always the feeling that I was being outmaneuvered, but this time the evidence was with me. "Do you admit that you have been peddling a purported cure for seasickness?" I said to the snuff-munching hickory farmer from Emory Gap, Tennessee. He looked at me with those popping blue eyes and finally in a hurt tone explained how his compassion for others always seemed to get him in trouble.

"Captain, these last four days of storm have put our boys through a lot of misery," he began. "Couple of them were threatening to jump overboard. That wouldn't look good in your 201, either." Already, I was beginning to feel uneasy.

Snuffy continued, "My Grandma, Gracie Bedford Houston, had a vision. She could see me in a terrible storm at sea and in her sweet way sent me two gallons of the family time-tested seasick medicine. Been handed down for five generations—ever since we took Texas from the Mexicans. A proud thing for the Bedford-Houston clan."

"Wait a minute," I said. "Emory Gap is nine-hundred miles from the ocean. Why would your family ever need a seasick remedy?"

Snuffy brightened. "Of course, you wouldn't know because you've never been to Emory Gap. Every house in that town has a front porch swing. There's not a movie house or bar within buggy distance of Emory and after chores everybody sits on those swings and rocks until it is time for bed. Why, when Uncle Hickory Jackson broke his big toe while climbing out of the corn crib, he sat and rocked in that swing for eight straight hours. Neighbors thought he was dead and that the wind was blowing him back and forth.

"Well, when I saw the misery our boys were in I knew I had to do something. It was heartbreaking to see some of them leaning over the rail, into the wind, and everything coming back. I knew then that Grandma Gracie would want me to share and help them find a little peace and comfort. It was her part in the war effort. Bless her."

"What's in this miracle cure-all?" said Fabian.

"Granny would be upset if I tell you," Snuffy protested. "The exact mixture has been in the family for more than sixty years—sort of like the Coca Cola formula, but I know you gentlemen won't let it get out of this room." Then in a soft voice he said, "Watauga River branch water, Loosahatchie phosphate runoff, liquefied chicken droppings, and Chickamauga spindrift."

Fabian was aghast. "My God, I just drank a slug of landfill concentrate! How come it smells and tastes like vanilla extract?"

Snuffy looked puzzled for a second and then said, "Oh, that. The boys didn't like the taste of it, so to make it more palatable and cover the odor I added a drop of vanilla to each bottle."

"A drop!" Fabian said, "The only thing in the bottle I sampled that wasn't vanilla extract was the cork. More alcohol than a double manhattan at Tiger Joe's!"

Snuffy looked puzzled and hurt. "Somebody must have gotten mixed up and added more than one drop in a couple of bottles."

I asked who "somebody" was.

Snuffy squirmed a bit. "Daryl Lewis, the cook, helped me. We had to work fast. You know how quickly that storm was upon us. Daryl was a big help."

Fabian produced a requisition requesting nine cases of vanilla that I had signed before leaving San Diego. I had questioned the quantity but Daryl assured me he intended to do a lot of baking and would need every drop. "Holy stick buns!" said Fabian. "This is enough vanilla to take us through World War Three!"

Daryl Lewis had been a short-order cook in a Seventh Avenue New York drugstore where his specialty was fried bagels in onion sauce. When I asked about the excessive amount of vanilla extract he had requested he explained that he planned to provide our ship with the finest in gourmet baking—cakes, pies, cookies, sticky buns—a pastry menu to make the FS344 the envy of the fleet. "Remember, Captain," he said," a ship sails on its stomach." I had never read that in the seamanship manual.

Fabian was looking skeptical. "How come since leaving port all I've had to eat is Spam and jelly sandwiches? What happened to that five-star menu of baked goods?"

"That was a problem," said first-class baker Lewis. "You know, at sea there's a rule that says the enlisted crew gets fed first. Our boys, worn out by the storm, have been inhaling those pastries like they were going out of style. There was never enough left for the officers' mess."

Fabian rolled his eyes. "Now that the storm has pretty much abated, can we expect to start savoring some of your legendary bakery creations? The Captain has a birthday next week; it would be nice if you bake a double layer cake for him. His favorite."

Ignoring the sarcasm, Lewis shook his head. "That's the problem. We're down to our last half bottle of vanilla. Not enough to get us to where ever we're going. Guess it's back to the canned goods again."

There was another meeting with Snuffy. I emphasized that there would be serious charges against him. Also, that we knew he and Lewis were a conspiracy acting to distribute an alcoholic mixture to members of the crew, that there would be questions to answer which I hoped he was prepared for. Snuffy, with a grave and understanding look, thanked me for the warning and expressed a sincere hope that the board of inquiry would not be too harsh with me.

"Just a minute, Corporal," I said. "Don't you think you're going to get me involved. I'm the one who discovered your complicity. You're the one being charged, not me!"

Snuffy understood. With deep compassion he expressed complete agreement with my position. "We all know that you were no part of the caper, but will the board know that? You know those eager young JAG types. Some smart ass would-be lawyer who hasn't passed his bar exam is going to ask you why you approved a requisition for nine cases of vanilla extract to cover a ten-day voyage."

I began to sputter. "Why—what do I know about cooking—how do I know how much of the damn vanilla it takes to bake a cake? How do I know that the extract is ninety-eight-percent alcohol? I don't do the cooking—I run the ship!"

There was no response from Snuffy. He just sat there with those sad, bulging eyes looking like a chaplain about to administer last rites.

"Get back to your post," I croaked.

Fabian was of no help. "He's got a point," he said. "When that vanilla extract thing comes out we've going to look like refugees from a nursery school."

"What do we do?" I said.

I knew my smooth-tongued morale officer would have a solution. Fabian leaned forward and in a conspiratorial tone outlined a plan: "Let me confiscate Snuffy's remaining inventory of Mother Sills seasick remedy. Then we will search the galley and toss overboard any vanilla extract Lewis may have left. The crew will probably complain about not having happy-hour cocktails available, but that's their problem, not ours."

"What about the charges against Snuffy?"

"Forget them," said Fabian, "but don't tell his granny that he revealed the family's secret recipe for all that ails a lonely sailor. She might put the ancestral curse on him."

Several weeks later I thought to ask Fabian how he had disposed of Snuffy's remaining bottle of the magic elixir. Fabian tried to remember but the matter had slipped his mind. That same week Daryl Lewis, the cook, told me that Fabian had asked him several times if there were any olives aboard. "Why would Lt. Murphy suddenly decide he wanted olives?" he said.

"Beats me," I said. "Maybe he enjoys spitting the pits."

Chapter Thirteen

After we wandered more than thirty-five miles off course, Captain Drumond put the FS344 on a short leash. We were repositioned in the convoy so our station was directly astern the Millard Fillmore. The other seven ships were ordered to keep a watchful eye on us and report any deviance from our assigned position or course. Lt. Montgomery Morgan considered this "unnatural" surveillance as an invasion of privacy. "With binoculars they could watch me taking a shower," he said. "From now on I'm wearing my shorts, night and day. This is worse than prep school at Exeter."

Fabian was more pragmatic about our nosey neighbors at sea. "I don't give a damn about who sees me taking a shower. It's the poker game that worries me. Some holier–than–thou character may discover our morale building recreational game in the forward hold and want to close it down."

Fabian's efforts to keep the crew gainfully occupied during off-duty hours proved to be more gainful for him than anyone else. He and Snuffy combined their back-of-the-barber-shop talents to organize a round-the-clock poker game in the empty number one hold. The gods of chance seemed to favor one of the two on alternate nights. When Fabian lost, Snuffy appeared to be the winner. Neither of the two complained about their losses. They were both good sports, although Fabian groused about the limited market—only sixteen in the crew available to participate in their friendly gatherings.

After five days out, Captain Drumond decided it was safe to tell us our destination—the Marshall Islands, where the Marines had just secured Kwajalein and Eniwekok. Our assignment would be to ferry in supplies and personnel from the deep-draft ships lying offshore. It was a relief to me to learn that this was non-combative duty, inasmuch as I had never completed basic training or fired anything more lethal than a starter's pistol. Lt. Fabian Murphy was pleased. "Now, maybe we can meet some other guys interested in a little recreational poker," he said.

After eleven days at sea, we reached the Marshals and anchored a half-mile off Kwajalein. For the first time, we saw signs of war. Disabled, abandoned landing craft littered the harbor, and weapons of all sizes were still scattered about the beach bearing witness to the recent struggle of determined Marines trying to find a foothold on a stretch of unforgiving sand, while a hidden enemy, sworn never to surrender, decimated American ranks, some still sloshing through the surf. It was sobering to a group of non-combative warriors who, a few days earlier, had been arguing about which one had finished off the last can of strawberry ice cream.

Our first assignment was an emotional experience that bordered on traumatism for a few of the crew. Those ingenious Navy Seabees had constructed a floating pier enabling small ships to come alongside for loading. We were ordered to pick up wounded Marines and transfer them to a hospital ship that lay in deep water a mile off the coast. None of us were prepared for what we saw. The movies, in Hollywood style, had shown us that wounded soldiers are usually neatly bandaged, smoking a cigarette, and wisecracking with attractive nurses. This time the script wasn't being followed. We were taking on board still-breathing bags of flesh and bones, some begging to be finished off, others without arms, legs, eyes, some unable to communicate or beg for anything. For the first time we realized that war wasn't a USO dance with thunder in the distance.

Snuffy was the only crewman who did not appear to be affected. He had seen it all during the first World War. Noticing my unnatural pallor, he took me aside and softly said, "Use it all up now, skipper. Next time it won't bother you. Next time you will just be mad. Mad because it had to happen."

"But I feel so helpless," I said. "There's nothing I can do for these guys who a few days ago were just like me, except braver. Now they are almost nonexistent, unimportant—a zero in a world that wants to know what can you do for me tomorrow. Right now, I feel like the inadequate one. What can I do for them?"

"Nothing for them," said Snuffy. "But think of the ones who will probably be torn apart this same way a couple of decades from now. Maybe you can do something about that."

Like what?

"By doing your part to help convince the world that everything that hurts comes from greed," said Snuffy. "Without greed there wouldn't be war. Of course, without war I don't know where I'd be. Probably in jail somewhere."

"Wait a minute," I said "What about that twenty-four-hour poker game you and Fabian are running in the number one hold? Isn't there some greed involved there?"

For a moment Snuffy looked chagrined, and then, in almost a whisper, he said, "I guess greed will always be with us."

Fabian Murphy was more stoic about greed.

"If it presents itself, you condemn it, give it another name, and use it to your advantage. The poker game is morale-building recreation for servicemen half a world away from home."

Our close association with other ships, both Army and Navy, provided an enlarged market for Fabian's social hours. Sailors were visiting the FS344 daily during off-duty periods for sessions of fraternization and games of skill.

On an afternoon after three runs into Eniwetok, we saw a small launch powered by an outboard motor approaching the port boarding ladder. Standing at the bow was a neat figure in Navy tans. On his collar was a small silver cross.

Fabian was alarmed. "Damn it, it's a chaplain. Someone has squealed about the poker table. Let me handle him."

I was pleased to delegate this authority.

Stepping smartly into the well deck, the young officer saluted the ensign and then raised his eyes toward the sky "Protect this valiant ship, O Lord, and watch over the brave crew that mans it. Keep them safe so they may return to their homes and loved ones. Amen." We were moved, even Snuffy, and echoed a respectful "amen" of our own.

Turning to me, the visiting chaplain began an apology. "Captain, I have been negligent. There are so many ships here it has been impossible to provide the regular attention and guidance that every serviceman has been promised. I should have called upon you weeks ago. Will you forgive me"? I told him that not only would we forgive him but if it would ease his schedule we would be willing to forgo his next couple of visits. He thanked me for this unselfish compassion toward others, but said we had sacrificed enough. He would not neglect our need of religious counseling and divine guidance.

As the good chaplain was about to leave, he turned back to me and with a slight frown said, "I have heard from others that someone aboard this ship is operating a game of chance. We both know that gambling is forbidden by God and the military. I hope you will tell me the rumor is false."

Fabian Murphy stepped forward. "Father, as morale officer I would like to explain that what we are doing is not gambling. It is a game of diversion to fight boredom and the temptation of evils we are familiar with—you probably heard that last week two native girls got aboard one of the anchored ships. Bad business, chaplain. That would never happen here. Our boys are involved in wholesome recreation during idle hours. Keeps their minds clear and their morals high."

The chaplain was still unconvinced. "But money changes hands, doesn't it? Don't some players win money at the expense of others? The Bible forbids that, you recall. Remember the money-changers in the temple?"

Fabian smiled. "Father, the military won't issue us chips—ping pong balls, yes, but no poker chips. So we improvise by using coins of small denominations just to keep track of things.
At the end of the week we average out and no one seems to lose anything. Why don't you see for yourself? Join us for a hand or two and you'll see how valuable this harmless recreation can be."

The chaplain hesitated, then said, "I supposed it would be a way to convince myself that there is some soundness to your argument, but what would be the reaction of the corps if it was discovered that I had participated in a card game? By the way, call me Timothy. That is the name assigned to me by the Order."

Fabian was warming up. "Father Timothy, you have the honor of this ship to rely on. Word that you conducted this investigation to separate right from wrong will never leave the number one hold. If it is your decision that this is gambling in the evil sense of the word, it will be shut down. If you decide it is healthful recreation, we will dedicate a portion of the winnings to the Servicemen Dependents Welfare Fund—I know that is a favorite charity of the Chaplains Corps."

That did it. "Apparently this will be the only way I can determine the real purpose of this questionable activity," said the chaplain. "Keep in mind, my decision in the matter will be final. If I disapprove, the game is over. I will report it to commanding headquarters and request appropriate charges. I will be available tomorrow. What time is the game?"

"Anytime, "said Fabian." It never stops."

The chaplain's launch driver appeared to become impatient. His motions implied that it was time to leave. As they moved out across the harbor toward the Seabee installation on the larger island, the Army mail boat came alongside to deliver fruit cake and word from home.

After our guest departed I asked Fabian about his modus operandi. It sounded hazardous to me. Fabian winked. "Don't you get the big picture?" he said. "After a few games we clean him out. He's at least a captain with a few bucks to lose. The last time he played cards it was Old Maid at divinity school. When he realizes that he has lost everything but his good conduct medal and begins to complain is when I pull the ace from my sleeve. I regretfully report that one
of the players who lost money is now threatening to spread the word that the very Reverend Timothy had become a gambler aboard one of the ships. And that only I can keep that information from getting out. He will be so intimidated he will deny ever seeing us or our poker game."

Chaplain Timothy arrived alongside at exactly 1630, nervous and with apparent misgivings. The poker players, four from neighboring ships, were gathered in the hold all cued to the fleecing about to begin. The chaplain had may questions about the game. Were aces high or low? What was a face card? Before taking his place he questioned Fabian about the winnings percentage that would go to the welfare fund, pointing out that he understood this game would be so innocent there would be no winnings. So there would be something for the fund, why not five percent of each hand's ante? "Otherwise it will be against my principles to participate," he said.

Fabian stiffened, but finally agreed, adding that the word is "pot" and the takeout is called "rake." Then the chaplain asked if his launch driver could be allowed in the game. "Poor fellow, sitting out there in that bobbing boat is pretty monotonous duty. Doesn't know much about poker, but then you've told me nobody really loses at these games." Fabian agreed. One more patsy is always welcome, he thought.

The game began. Some of the players were a little uneasy playing against a man with a silver cross on his collar. The real problem was trying to keep him from losing. He exposed his hidden cards before the others had placed their bets. Why was a straight better than a flush? Did a call have to be loud? At the end of the game, the chaplain was ahead four dollars. His launch driver was down two dollars. The only winner seemed to be the Welfare Fund. After each hand, the chaplain clumsily counted out five percent of pot and raked it into a canvas bag. As the money dropped into the bag he would say a short prayer and bless all those who had contributed.

As Chaplain Timothy left the ship he told Fabian that he still was not convinced that the game was pure recreation and not gambling. "I'll be back tomorrow and try to determine whether or not someone is rigging the game to make it appear innocent and without the evil of chance," he said.

The next day the chaplain arrived late and explained there was a problem obtaining gasoline for the launch. His coxswain joined the game again and seemed to have learned how to shuffle the cards in a more professional manner. The chaplain had not improved and kept trying to claim that two pair were greater than three of a kind. It was difficult to keep him from losing big money. Like the previous game, money moved around the table without anyone seeming to win a worthwhile pot. He was pleased and said he regretted that tomorrow would be our last game for a while. Word was out that we were soon going to be moved to the Gilbert Islands, but he hoped we could continue our research there.

Fabian began setting up the sting. Four crewmen from the Tiapa planned to join the shearing. "Tomorrow, our chaplain will not only go home broke but he will feel so guilty about his part in a gambling orgy that he will never mention poker again," said Fabian. "Tomorrow, we're playing for keeps."

When the game began, there was unusually active signal traffic in the anchorage. The chaplain's launch driver appeared nervous and was raising pot bets in a reckless fashion. The chaplain kept asking stupid questions like was a royal flush better than a ten-high straight, and still dropping his cards on the deck. His driver seemed to be doing better. Momentarily, luck was with the chaplain. When he would lay out a full house after his driver had built up the pot beyond normal limits, and ask if his hand was worth anything. "Beginner's luck," muttered Fabian under his breath. Money began changing hands so fast no one was sure where it was going. Snuffy had to borrow fifty dollars from the cook to stay in the game. Fabian was beginning to panic. He winked at Snuffy indicating it was time for the cleaver to fall. Snuffy looked helpless. After apologizing for laying down three queens and a pair of aces, the chaplain raked the pot into his canvas bag and announced that all his winnings would go to the Welfare Fund. His driver won the next three hands and said that he would donate fifty percent of his take to the chaplain's charity. "God will be pleased," said the chaplain.

Just then our signalman rushed in with a message from the Fillmore. All personnel to return to their stations immediately. All ships prepare to sail within forty minutes. We were on our way to the Gilbert Islands.

The chaplain was devastated. "We can't quit now. The winnings must be divided more equitably." He turned to Fabian. "Promise me you will continue this game at the first opportunity we have to meet." Fabian nodded numbly. The driver gathered up the two swollen bags, assisted the chaplain into the launch, and we watched Father Timothy wave a blessing to all of us.

Like a mother hen, Captain Drumond on the Fillmore spent the next two hours rounding up his chicks and assigning us our positions in the convoy. Dodging Drumond's imaginary submarines, it took four days to reach the Gilberts. For the following two weeks we worked around the clock, off-loading supplies from the transports and bringing out wounded. Fabian was fretting. "Unless we get some free time the poker game will fall apart and we will never recover our money from that lucky God-fearing chaplain," he protested. "Right now he is probably trying to convince some brass hat that it's time to bless our ship again. Poor sucker doesn't realize that he hit a lucky steak he'll never see again. This time we will take him and the Welfare Fund, too. Anybody who doesn't know how many cards in a deck should stick to church-night bingo."

After three weeks, support activity began to slow up. We went back to regular watches with time to do laundry and write home for more fruitcake. A lone Japanese aircraft made some threatening passes but was driven off by the Fillmore's aircraft guns. Lt. Montgomery Morgan, eager to be an item in the Morgan's glorious family tradition of defending their country ever since the American revolution, raced to the top of the bridge and began firing the port side fifty caliber machine gun at the disappearing enemy plane. His first bursts barely missed lookout Elwood Corbin, still at his duty station on the bow. As he swung the barrel in the general direction of the fleeing pilot, Lt. Morgan cut down the Tiapa's emergency radio antenna before getting the tail of the rapidly diminishing plane in his sights.

The stimulation of combat caused Monty to forget everything he had been told about rapid-firing automatic weapons—that air-cooled guns must be fired only in bursts or the heat produced by continuous firing would cause the barrel to melt. This basic principle of metallurgy came to his attention when the gun stopped firing and he noticed that the barrel, like a limp pretzel, was pointed at the deck at a forty-degree angle. Our Japanese adversary could report to his commander that without firing a shot he had taken out one third of the FS344's armament. Not bad for an afternoon.

Now that the poker game was back in operation, Snuffy and Fabian were anxiously watching the anchorage area for signs of Chaplain Timothy. The only visitor we received was Captain Roger Drumond, who came aboard to inspect the damaged machine gun and suggest that it might be prudent to remove all weapons from the FS344 before we committed wholesale hari-kari. He was red-faced from climbing the Jacob's ladder and sputtering. "Do you realize that your air-headed first mate came close to wiping out the Tiapa!" he shouted. "Sure, she's an old coal burner, but certainly deserves more than being put down by her own kind. Put boxing gloves on that man before he tries to wind up the compass. Don't let him near anything smaller than a sea anchor."

Monty Morgan stood by listening to Captain Drumond's tirade and peering at the rotund Navy man through thick lens glasses and with understanding. "Poor man is suffering battle fatigue. We may have a caretaker's position for him at the estate after the war," he whispered to second mate, Darrow. It was a logical time to change the discussion and I was relieved when Fabian Murphy stepped forward and asked the Captain if he would arrange a visit from the group chaplain. "Some of the crew are homesick and need spiritual consoling. A visit of a couple of hours with the chaplain would lift our spirits," he said. "I know he must be busy but a short time with us would improve morale."

Captain Drumond looked puzzled. "What chaplain?" he said. "We don't have a chaplain. This outfit of misfits is lucky to get mail from home. Which reminds me that the commandant of the Seabees at Kwajalein wants to know why we tried to kidnap a couple of his men. Says they were AWOL from the base for three days because one of the ships they were visiting wouldn't let them leave, and then tried to sail with them aboard. Awful time trying to get away until a passing launch took them aboard. Sounds to me like somebody has been chewing too many betel nuts. Wildest story I've ever heard."

Fabian looked pale. "Were they moved to the Gilberts with the rest of us?" he asked.

"Not a chance," said Drumond. "There is enough rebuilding in the Marshals to keep the Seabees there for the duration. One is supposed to be a card shark. His mates call him Texas Tim—comes from San Antonio."

As he was leaving the ship, Captain Drumond spoke to Fabian Murphy quietly." I will see what I can do about digging up a chaplain, Lieutenant. I know how important it is to keep the faith."

"Thank you, sir, but don't bother," said Fabian.

Lost at sea

No problem — we're on water

Still Lost

Lost Again

The Captain at Ease

We're not lost

FS 344 at rest

Lieutenant Colonel William T. Melms

Chapter Fourteen

As first mate and navigating Officer, Lt. Montgomery Morgan spent most of his time trying to determine where we were. Usually it was a case of where we had been. By the time Monty had settled on an acceptable fix, it was several hours after his last observation, so by late afternoon we always knew where we had been at breakfast. Inept as Monty seemed to be about handling practical matters, like walking across the deck without tripping over a scupper, he was astute enough to recognize a con man when he saw one. As the scion of a New England family that traced its roots back to Cotton Mather, this scrawny apparition of a revolutionary minuteman had been taught to protect and preserve the family fortune at all cost. It appeared to the rest of us that learning how to live in luxury without ever dipping into the principal was his major at Harvard. It was logical that he would see in Lt. Fabian Murphy, financial wizard from South Boston, a man who could triple your wealth by turning cash into questionable paper.

"Lace-curtain Irish," Monty would snort.

"Over-educated, interbred aristocrat whose idea of a great pinup would be Betsy Ross in red flannel underwear," Fabian would respond.

Finally, the two stopped speaking—until the day Montgomery Morgan fell overboard.

It was in the New Guinea area off Salamana where the ship was unable to get within a quarter mile of shore. We were unloading supplies onto a lighter. Monty and Fabian were supervising but, as usual, not speaking to each other. Monty was standing at the port railing, looking aloft trying to identify the genus classification of a purple seagull he had just spotted. At that moment one of the rigging guys let go, causing the boom to sway and set up a pendulum action that sent the block across the deck, sweeping the pensive Lt. Morgan over the rail and into the sea.

Fabian rushed to the rail and looked down on a thrashing Montgomery breaking the surface for the second time and screaming for help. It appeared that Monty's double indemnity was about to pay off. Fabian was wondering how he could organized a quick pool based on the number of times Monty would resurface before disappearing forever. But he didn't have a chance to peddle a single ticket: the pendulum action of the free-swinging boom carried the block to starboard and then returned it to port and hit Fabian over the side—he splashed next to the floundering Monty. Fabian could swim. Snuffy, who had been operating the winch motors, threw a ring preserver onto the two struggling amphibians. Fabian grabbed one side of the ring and began to tow it off when Monty's flailing hand caught the other side and became part towee.

The crew lowered a breeches buoy and hauled the two officers' back to the deck. Monty Morgan lay spouting seawater like an over-hydrated porpoise.

Fabian's fake Rolex had stopped running and he was blaming Monty for having been studying seagulls instead of keeping his head down.

Corporal Corbin applied his CPR training until Monty begged for mercy. His first words were, "Let me talk to the brave person who saved me."

Snuffy said, "I tossed the ring"—Fabian stepped forward. "I had no choice. When a fellow human's life is at risk there is no room for consideration of personal safety. I would have leaped in the sea to save you even if there had been no life ring available. Childish, personal grievances become unsignificant in the face of death."

For a moment Monty thought he was still under water. "You! You saved me?" he croaked.

"We are all God's children," said Fabian, "responsible for each other. Any thanks should go to Him who propelled me over the rail to your side. I was just an instrument of His will."

Someone had found Monty's spare pair of coke-bottle-lens glasses and he peered through them with some suspicion. Then, without hesitation, he thrust out his hand. "I am deeply grateful for the risk you took to save the last of the Morgan line. The family will be forever indebted to you. You deserve an award. Could you use a lifetime membership in the Cape Cod Yacht Club? With our influence in the area we could get you in, you know—even if you are Irish."

Fabian dropped his head in embarrassment. "I deserve nothing. I was only following God's orders. You provided the opportunity for me to find myself. You risked your life so that I might prove that I was ready when the call came. You, Monty, deserve the award and I intend to do something for you. I mean it."

Monty coughed and expelled another half-pint of salt water. "What can you do for me?" he said, with the expression of an incredulous aristocrat who had just been offered food for work.

Fabian was ready. "There's nothing much I can do in a substantive way, but I can pass on to you an opportunity I was saving for an elderly aunt who raised me in South Boston. My associates at home are holding in my name one thousand shares of a company about to go IPO at thirty-six dollars. Insiders know that within ninety days of the offering it will triple in value. That's why so few of us have this initial option to buy. I want you, Monty Morgan, to accept this opportunity from me as a token of my appreciation for your sacrifice in helping me to be born again. It's the only thing I can offer."

"What's the name of the company?"

Fabian hesitated, leaned close, and whispered, "Paragon Slide Rules, Limited."

"Slide rules," said Monty. "Is there a demand for slide rules?"

"Not right now," said Fabian, "but as soon as the war is over every returning GI is going to want a slide rule, and Paragon is one of only three slide rule makers in the world. Every soldier can see how the military relies on slide rules. Biggest demand since can openers."

"What about your aunt?" said Monty. "I hate to deprive her of what could be a small fortune."

"It would be a token to her," said Fabian. "She doesn't need the money, and would probably be gone when it pays off. I know you don't need the money either, but think how pleased the estate will be to realize this substantial addition to the family principal."

That seemed to do it. "I accept," said Monty. "I'll write the trust and have them transfer thirty-six thousand dollars to your account. I still feel guilty about the entire matter but if it will ease your conscience it's all worth while."

Five weeks later a gold-edged certificate in the name of Montgomery Morgan III arrived. Monty said he would probably contribute the profits to some charity in the name of Fabian Murphy.

Watching Fabian's skill in the scam was embarrassing. I cornered him in the wardroom the day after the near drowning. "How could you in good conscience, create such a fraudulent scheme to the disadvantage of a fellow officer?"

Fabian said, "Some people are destined to be great leaders while others are here to be fleeced—or, as in the food chain, to be eaten." He held out his hands. "And I'm here to be one of the eaters before someone hungrier eats me."

"But slide rules?" I said, "We both know that there's work being done on the development of a hand-held calculator. Just a matter of time until slide rules will be as dead as buggy whips. You just peddled a sure loser."

Fabian shrugged. "Look, it's not all profit for me. That Paragon paper cost me seven dollars a share. Seven thousand bucks I can't afford."

"But Monty's into it for thirty-six thousand dollars," I said. "Not a bad markup for you. And I have a feeling somebody is paying you a healthy commission to move those losers even at seven dollars."

Fabian smiled. "Don't sweat it. Monty's exchequer back on Martha's Vineyard probably thinks he is stocking up on post cards. After the war we will never see each other again, and by the time he discovers slide rules are collectable antiques he will remember me only as the guy who saved him from drowning."

"But you didn't save him," I said. "You were busy saving your own skin dragging the life ring with you. If Monty hadn't unintentionally grabbed the hand line on the other side of the ring, we would be dragging the bottom for him right now."

"No big loss," said Fabian. "The family would have mounted a bronze plaque on the windward side of Plymouth rock telling how he saved the world for the Republicans. But I gave him a chance to be grateful and the knowledge that somebody cared enough to risk life for him."

"You would make John D. Rockefeller proud," I said.

It was four months later when we reached the Philippines and learned that no good deed goes unpunished. Communications back to the States was improving. We could depend on mail every ten days. Monty was getting his Harvard alumni bulletin and Fabian was beginning to hear from the boys in the Boston boiler room. Life was becoming easier for all of us—until February 10, 1945, when Fabian received the news about Paragon slide rules.

He burst into my quarters. "He's done it again!" he cried. "That miserable excuse for a patriot has swindled me! Monty Morgan should be brought before the mast and charged with larceny in the service!" He shoved a crumpled page from the Wall Street Journal into my face. "Read it and see for yourself."

The lead article was about Paragon Slide Ruler. The company had just been awarded a contract from the War Department to produce 15,000 mini-gyros, a sensational new development in direction-finding equipment to be installed in tanks and jeeps as well as in the back packs of foot soldiers in the field. Allied nations were already clamoring for them. The company had announced it was closing out the slide rule division to concentrate on the production of portable gyro compasses. Analysts were predicting a windfall for Paragon shareholders. General Electric and Westinghouse were competing with each other to take over the company.

"Those thousand shares could be worth a million," said Fabian. "Monty has no right to all that. I deserve a healthy finder's fee. I'm going to demand it. After all, who kept that pretentious scarecrow from drowning?"

"I think it was Snuffy," I said.

At that moment, Lt. Monty Morgan, accompanied by officers Baldwin and Darrow, came into the room. "Have you heard the word on Paragon Slide Rules?" he said. "Fabian was so right. Shares have more than tripled. They say those thousand shares may be worth a million!" He turned to Fabian. "Old friend, you've more than vindicated my trust in you. I knew that when you said you were born again after the near tragedy when I was swept overboard, God would be our broker in the Paragon investment. He continues to watch over the both of us."

Fabian groaned.

Lt. Monty Morgan continued. "I am not a selfish person. I am not going to keep this small fortune. I am going to share every dollar with those who are more deserving."

Fabian brightened. "I knew we could count on you to do the right thing, Monty. How are you going to spread it?"

Monty peered through the coke-bottom lenses of his glasses at each of us and then, with the modest smile of a kindly benefactor said, "I am not entitled to any of that money." Fabian nodded in agreement. Monty continued, "I agreed to accept Fabian's offer only to help relieve him of the guilt that probably plague all Irishmen of questionable ancestry. True to his amazing financial knowledge, the investment has multiplied in value many times and now is the time to cast our bread on the water."

"You're right, Monty," said Fabian. "Which direction are we going cast the baked goods?"

With look of a Salvation Army captain at Christmas, Montgomery Morgan made his announcement. "I am going to use all of the profits from this fortuitous investment to build a retirement home in Cantine, Maine, for the Sons of the American Revolution. Think what this will mean to those heirs of the early patriots who now find themselves unable to afford the comforts of living they so richly deserve." He smiled at Fabian. "And for you, my friend, a special honor. I will name the place Fabian J. Murphy Home of the Patriots. Don't try to thank me. You are entitled to the honor. Without the humility that prompted you to make that initial proposal, all this would not be possible. As soon as we are all back home, you will be requested to attend the groundbreaking ceremony, to be recognized and thanked. I'm sure you and your family will be there."

"I can hardly wait," said Lt. Fabian J. Murphy.

How to Stay Afloat Wearing Army Boots

Chapter Fifteen

Military orders leave nothing to possible misinterpretation or the imagination of a recipient looking for ways to avoid inconvenient duty. Officer-training programs include a three-week course on writing military orders. Special emphasis is put on "will," a word that implies that if you *don't* expect big problems even a court-martial could lead to unpleasant things, like execution.

At Fort Eustis, Virginia, I shared a room with a young Jewish officer who had never celebrated a Christian holiday. He was disconcerted when our post commander issued a holiday order wishing each of us a Happy New Year, ending with the greeting of "You *will* have a Merry Christmas."

Lt. Frankel was perplexed. "How can I have a merry day that my religion doesn't recognize?" he said, "But if I don't, I'll be disobeying a direct order."

We took the matter to Captain Nails who was in his first year of law school when the Army grabbed him. After two Canadian Clubs at the officers' mess, Addison Nails was ready with an opinion. "It's just a matter of subterfuge," he said. "On December 25, if you run into the post commander at the club or anywhere else on the post, smile. Even laugh if he tells one of his dumb stories about the Egyptian girls at Port Said. But don't take chances. Smile at all people, even if you don't like them. You know how word travels. If someone sees you frowning and looking miserable, headquarters will hear about it and you will be called before the mast to explain your willful disobedience of a direct order. You maybe hurting on the inside, but a happy face will keep your record clean." Barrister Nails added another Canadian Club to his fee. "This time with a twist of lemon," he said.

The first "you will" order I tried to dodge occurred when Bob Hope and a USO troupe arrived at our anchorage near Morotai Island. The Marines had been moving from island to island on their drive toward the Philippines. We trailed along, picking up the pieces, trying not to feel guilty about our non-combative role in recapturing the South Pacific while those gallant leathernecks moved from one invasion area to another risking everything without hesitation. We were busy. Most of us had been without rest for more than 36 hours. Now, while the Marines were regrouping for their next push, it appeared we would have an opportunity for sack time and writing home for more crumbled cookies. Before I could get my soggy deck shoes off, the message from Capt Drumond arrived informing us that Bob Hope and a USO Company were arriving and would entertain the troops in the area at 1930 hours on the flight deck of the Intrepid. This was great news. I could skip the show and catch up on all that missing sleep. I had overlooked the part of the order that read, "You will attend."

Lt. Fabian Murphy also decided to pass up the show, but for a different reason. As I recalled, prior to the war he had peddled some worthless shares of Essence of Apricot Pits to Mr. Hope when the entertainer was passing through Boston and had the misfortune of taking one of Fabian's telephone calls. "How did I know that Congress would slap a moratorium on the efficiency of its curative powers?" said the former boiler room executive. "In good faith, I was trying to double his investment. We were both victims of circumstances beyond our control."

"How come you didn't buy any?" I said. Fabian ignored the question.

When Capt. Drumond learned that two of his officers would not be attending the show, he came launching over to our ship, livid and ready to explicate the chain of command to us.

"Did you read your orders?" he bellowed. "Please note, gentlemen, the words 'you *will* attend a USO performance featuring Mr. Robert Hope on the flight deck of USN Aircraft Carrier Intrepid at 1930 hours'."

He glared at us for a moment, then continued. "This man has traveled almost three-thousand miles to entertain you and to bring brief relief from the drudgery of military duty. Now you see fit to affront him and decline his compassionate offer to make your life at sea a little more bearable."

"But I haven't had any sleep for two days," I said. "I'll probably fall asleep during the performance."

Capt. Drumond stood closer. "Mister, apparently you don't understand the seriousness of this matter. However, I will report to the area commander that it is your decision to disobey a direct order."

"We will be there," I said.

He smiled. "Good decision. Also, after the show there will be a reception for Mr. Hope with just the officers present. We expect you to attend that, too. Each of us will have the privilege to shake his hand and express our appreciation."

Fabian Murphy groaned.

The flight deck of the Intrepid was a sea of sailors in their dress whites. Our group of five small Army vessels provided a minority of forty soldiers, conspicuous in their drab khaki uniforms, uncomfortably outnumbered by their service rivals. Bob Hope noticed the disparity and cracked that the government must have discovered a few soldiers of no value on earth so it put them on water. Naval Captain Drumond nodded in agreement. Hope's problem was with the audience's premature anticipation of the punch line: before he could reach the point of the joke, the entertainment starved sailors hooted until the rigging rattled. It was rough on Bob's timing.

Following the show, thirty-six officers, including five from our ship, filed into the carrier's wardroom to meet Bob Hope. Fabian was nervous and tried to dodge the reception line, but, like a good shepherd, Capt. Drumond kept his charges in formation. There was no way to avoid shaking the hand of the famous comedian.

Monty Morgan, heir to most of New England and a net worth close to Hope's own, was a typical down east stoic who found it difficult to discern anything worthwhile in a comedy program. When his place in line reached the guest of honor, he squinted through those wire-rim magnifying glasses and asked Bob Hope why, so far into the reception, he had said nothing funny.

Bob became very serious. "It's the cost," he said. "Do you realize how much I pay for every joke I use? There were over eight-hundred men on the flight deck. The joke cost per man was within reason, but here, with fewer than thirty-six people, the gag cost would be more than I could afford. Besides, within forty-eight hours the punch lines would have spread throughout the fleet and become obsolete. So, for economic reasons, no jokes off duty."

Monty looked at Hope with new admiration. Spoken like a true New Englander.

Fabian was not eager for his part of the line to reach the genial entertainer. Shaking his hand, Bob Hope peered closely at him and said, "Haven't I seen you somewhere before? Some guy in Boston with a name like yours once sold me sixty-thousand dollars worth of wallpaper. Couldn't be you, could it?"

A crestfallen Fabian Murphy looked deeply hurt.

"Sir," said Fabian. "There are a great many Murphys in Boston. Most of them, like myself, are upright, respected citizens. Hardworking people whose objective in life is the preservation of this great country, regardless of personal sacrifice. Helping others, my family and community, has shaped my life."

Hope looked dubious. "The Irishman who conned me with apricot pits didn't help me much. He was shaping things, all right—mostly his own bank account. Sure you don't know anything about it?"

"Shamefully, sir, there are always back-sliders in every group. Unfortunately, I bear the name of a second cousin from Cork who left Erie under questionable conditions. You may have run into him, although I'm reasonably sure he had the best of intentions to better your financial position. As a Certified Financial Planner, I would never suggest anything so speculative as uranium."

"You're a Certified Financial Planner?" said Hope.

"Yes, sir," said Fabian. "Spend most of my time advising churches, charitable fundraisers, and consulting with endowment committees. It's gratifying work."

"What's in it for you?" said Hope.

"Satisfaction," said Fabian, "knowing that in a small way I am assisting deserving people help themselves. I would be happy to look over your portfolio and offer what I can to help you increase the net and avoid taxes. No fee, of course. It's the least I can do to offset that unfortunate experience you suffered with an unscrupulous member of the Murphy clan."

Bob Hope was moved, but hesitating. "Nice of you to offer," he said. "I guess we show people need all the help we can find. I'll get back to you."

In the launch returning to our ship, Fabian was smug about his evening's accomplishments. "He's ready to take the bait," he said. "Can you imagine being a financial advisor to a guy with money coming out of his ears! This is like a whale swimming through a school of minnows."

Late the next afternoon, Capt. Drumond came storming aboard. "You've embarrassed me, the Army Transportation Corps, and the entire fleet!" When his jowls began to quiver and his earlobes turned red, we knew the old salt was agitated. "First of all, those two Greek Lotharios of yours, privates Aristotle and Matlaxis, cornered one of those cutie backup girl singers and convinced her they were movie producers back in Greece. Then they bedded her down with the promise to make her a Greta Garbo when they got home. Worse, she's notified Mr. Hope that she's leaving the troupe to go home and brush up on her Greek accent! If that isn't bad enough, Mr. Hope did some rapid research on your financial guru, Lt. Fabian Murphy. Says we should string him up from the nearest yardarm. It seems that Seaman Murphy in the boiler room screwed him out sixty-thousand dollars two years ago and now wants to handle his financial affairs! It was also noted that the soldiers from our flotilla displayed a lack of appreciation for this outstanding USO performance. Your crew, particularly, were not notably enthusiastic and let the Navy out-laugh you on every joke. What's your explanation?"

"Maybe we were sleepy," I said.

"Can't win them all," added Fabian.

Chapter Sixteen

"The PR for this ship stinks!" said Barry Darrow. Third mate Lt. Darrow earned a degree in marketing from Michigan State with emphasis on communications and corporate public relations. When he joined the Army, officer procurement promised him an assignment as a civilian liaison promoting war bonds and convincing the home front that every commander was the greatest military strategist since Napoleon Bonaparte, except for General Douglas MacArthur, who exceeded even the feat of Moses parting the Red Sea. It was a grave disappointment when the dapper Darrow found himself aboard an Army boat that bobbed up and down like a hobby horse so continuously that he spent most of his duty time hanging over the leeward rail. "Nobody knows what in the hell we are," he said. "We've got to have some publicity that will enhance our image. Even my mother tells her friends that I'm a Naval officer aboard an aircraft carrier. She won't show them my picture in that Army-drab uniform. I know how I got here. When I filled out the background check form, I mentioned being an afternoon canoe rental manager while going to school. That triggered 'water experience' and I was bingoed out to the Army's marine division. If I am ever going to be remembered for contributing anything to the winning of the war in the South Pacific, we need attention."

"We could keel-hawl Monty Morgan," said Fabian Murphy. "That would get the attention of the DAR who would probably claim that it was a loyalist plot to get revenge for the Morgan clan's part in the American Revolution."

"This isn't a time for comedy," said Darrow. "Right now the only things we're noted for is the time we sank a friendly banana boat and when our talented skipper crashed two piers on the same day."

"I resent that," I said. "You guys forget that I had a staff that thought portside was a waterfront wine bar. And you, Lt. Darrow, refused to 'box' the compass because you were against violence. With a crew like this, who needs an enemy?"

It was apparent that everyone was beginning to feel like the school kid who was always chosen last to play on the scrub baseball team. Even Captain Drumond said that no enemy submarine captain would waste a twenty-five thousand dollar torpedo to sink a ship that might not bring that much on the scrap market. Of course, Captain Drumond was biased and felt that without the Army messing things up the war would be shortened by six months. We suspected that he secretly hoped the entire crew of the FS344 would be charged with gross incompetence and sentenced to a listening post on a hilltop in a remote part of Mindanao.

There seemed to be no answer to Darrow's complaint until Monty Morgan mentioned that the trust administrator for the Morgan estate was Addison Claywell, a long time friend of General MacArthur and his late father. When Darrow heard this he went into an orbit of excitement and PR ecstasy.

For more than three months we could smell eventual victory for the Allies. We were being moved from one captured island to another. Lt. Baldwin groused about the lack of time to complete the cataloging of his stamp collection. It appeared that General MacArthur's promise of "I will return" was about to be kept.

Lt. Darrow, in a style that would make his Michigan State public relations instructor proud, outlined the scenario that would end with a six-column halftone of the FS344 on the front page of the *New York Times*—if everything went well.

Monty Morgan was instructed to write Mr. Claywell immediately and request that he communicate with General Mac Arthur and suggest that he make his glorious return to the Philippines on an Army vessel. What could be more logical than an Army vessel carrying an Army General – commander of the Pacific Theatre – to his meeting with destiny on the shores of Leyte Island in the Philippines? This was assuming, of course, that we didn't get lost and land on enemy held territory. Also assuming that the FS344 would be the ship of his choice.

Lt. Baldwin was skeptical. "Why would this Claywell character be presumptuous enough to think he could tell the Supreme Commander how to make his triumphant return to the Philippines?"

"No problem," said Fabian Murphy. "The ace in the deck is the Morgan family trust. In his letter Monty mentions that after the war the Morgans plan to review the return on their trust, but he is reasonably certain there will be no change of handlers. The trust department will get the message fast and Addison Claywell will be on the tube in a hurry to get his friendly suggestion to the forward moving General and his media relations staff."

Monty was reluctant to involve the influence of the Morgan family, but finally agreed when it was settled that he would be watch officer on duty and personally conn the ship toward the beach on Leyte Island.

Monty's letter was a cooperative project that involved everyone except Monty who spent most of his free time polishing his brass and pressing his dress uniform. Snuffy was called upon to do the final editing and it was the little forty year corporal's touches that made the request sound logical.

"Everybody is a 'ham'," said Snuffy. "Play to that and you'll never hear 'no'."

The letter left for the States with the next dispatch and the entire crew began practicing for their brief moments of fame. Lt. Darrow wrote to his mother telling her to watch the newsreels for a big event in the South Pacific, soon to happen. Fabian was putting together a few investment opportunities that might interest the newsmen who would be interviewing him. Even our dedicated lookout, Elwood Corbin, began practicing to modulate his voice better so it would record clearly when he announced that General MacArthur was missing when he left the ship to wade through the surf.

For the first time, the cook began searching his recipe file for ways to prepare delicate fingertip snacks for the General to nibble on while he waited during our approach to the beach.

It was a heady time for us all, but there was no indication from anywhere that this image-building moment in history would ever take place.

It was forty days after Monty's letter left for the mainland when the first sign appeared that someone had heard of the FS344. Capt Drumond announced that he was coming aboard for his regular monthly inspection a week ahead of schedule. This was unusual because Drumond detested these visits as much as we did: he implied that we were on water because we were no good on earth. But now it was suspiciously different. He greeted the officer of the deck with a smile and commented on the neatness of his uniform. Even Elwood's ear-grating announcement of his arrival did not seem to annoy him. After a congenial tour of the ship he accepted, for the first time, our invitation to join us for lunch. Even complimented the cook, telling him he wished food this good was served on the Fillmore.

As Drumond was stepping down to his launch, he turned and mentioned the rumors that MacArthur would soon be returning to the Philippines. "Word is that the general is considering using an Army vessel to take him in. Be nice if it was one of ours." Capt. Drumond smartly saluted the ensign as the launch headed back to the Fillmore.

"He knows!" shouted Darrow. "The old bastard knows we've been selected and he won't tell us. From now on we'll get some respect from his damn fleet."

Fabian was thinking ahead. "We'll go down in history as the ship that paved the road to victory in the South Pacific! After the war the FS344 will be moored to a pier somewhere as a tourist attraction. People will pay to come aboard. They will read the bronze plaque with our names embossed in it. We'll be legends."

The entire crew began working around the clock to bring the ship up to blue-ribbon condition. For the first time the fifty-cal machine guns were field stripped and cleaned. The cook got rid of the dead roaches back of the stove. The chipping/painting detail worked so hard they came close to hammering holes in the hull.

Then came a brief message from command headquarters that we could expect a visit from a Major James DeWeese the next day. That was all, but we knew that our moment of fame was coming closer.

Major DeWeese was a no-nonsense military man. Stepping aboard and carefully avoiding the usual conviviality expected by most visitors of rank, he asked for a meeting with senior officers. In our case that meant all four of us. He declined the offer of a cigarette from Fabian, who nervously snuffed out his own. Without expression, Major DeWeese told us that high command – rolling his eyes heavenward – was considering utilizing an Army watercraft to convey the General within reasonable distance of the beach. We suspected that meant within range of newsreel cameras. He mentioned that a memo from MacArthur suggested the FS344 be inspected for possible consideration. I asked where he would like to begin his inspection – bow or the stern.

"Just the log. I would like to review the ship's log – alone," he said.

This was disappointing. All that scraping, painting, polishing and eyewash had no interest to the inspector. Just the log. Too bad we hadn't cleaned up the coffee stains on the cover. We settled the Major in the chart room with a pitcher of ice water and two pieces of Danish the cook had baked that morning for the occasion. As I left the room Major DeWeese got up and closed the door.

For the next two hours the rest of us fretted. Monty Morgan had started to bite his nails. "This man is a student," he said. "He's going to mark you down for every split infinitive, every misspelling or misplaced comma. Aren't you sorry you didn't remember 'i before e, except after c'? I know the type. We're cooked."

Fabian was more encouraging. "Hey, this guy is a faker. He has never been on a ship before. Doesn't know what to look for so he decides to read the log. All that garble doesn't make sense, anyway. Not even to you, Skipper, and you wrote it."

"Thanks for your support," I said. "But do me a favor, Fabian. Don't talk to this guy. One faker knows another."

After almost two hours Major DeWeese emerged from the chart room with a thick notebook under his arm. The Danish was untouched. "The log seems relatively complete, but the incidents mentioned are without much backup detail. You note that a Lt. Morgan fell overboard and almost drowned, but no reason or explanation. I see you ran aground in midday near Dry Tortugas, but that's all, 'ran aground.' There is nothing here that would call for a special inquiry, but I will check with the Water Division of the Transportation Command for a more detail history of the FS344. Thank you, gentlemen." He stepped into his launch without saluting the insignia.

"I told you he knows nothing about ships," said Fabian. "Only an Army grunt would forget to highball the ship's flag."

"I don't like it," said Snuffy. "Those record keepers in the Pentagon can kill more careers than the enemy. Don't buy your commendation ribbons yet."

"Nothing to worry about," said Darrow. "You heard him say that technically there was nothing wrong with the log."

It was a sad day in the Central Pacific when we spotted Capt. Drumond's launch coming toward our anchorage at top speed. Through the glasses we could see that Drumond's ears were beet red again. A very bad sign. As usual he tripped over the port scupper and we heard him mutter, "Damn tub."

His first words to us were those we had heard before: "You've done it again! Blown the only chance this missmatched fleet of mine will ever have to be recognized!"

Lt. Darrow was shocked. "What happened, sir? Is it serious? Maybe a misunderstanding. You know, mixed-up records?"

Drumond exploded. "Major DeWeese contacted the War Department for your records and found out the only thing this ship hasn't done is sink an allied aircraft carrier! Listen to this list of your accomplishments: Ran aground three times – all in daylight in good weather. Lost two eighteen-hundred dollar anchors. Collided with and sank an Ecuadorian banana boat. Entered into off limits area in Gulf of Mexico and sailed through center of US Navy firing practice operation with grave risk to life and government property. Became lost twice while sailing with convoy crossing South Pacific. Disrupted Panama Canal traffic by entering locks stern first. Damaged piers at Pensacola and Panama City. Suspected of operating a shipboard brothel for two days while crossing Gulf of Mexico. Conducted illegal poker game in No. 1 hold until stopped by Chaplain Corps."

Capt. Drumond, face redder than ever, stopped to catch his breathe, "That's only half of your misbegotten history. Worst of all, you insulted Bob Hope!"

Monty Morgan, having trouble with his government – issue hearing aid, asked, "Will we still be allowed to take General MacArthur ashore?"

Capt. Drumond stared at the scrawny Lieutenant, scion of New England's rich and powerful, and with admirable control spoke softly: "Mister Morgan. General MacArthur is planning a dramatic return. He does not want to be stuck on a sand bar somewhere while you and your fellow officers argue about which way is North. He will go in aboard a Higgins Landing Craft piloted by a capable US Navy quartermaster. Thanks to you and your mates, the Army will have no part in the operation."

Fabian Murphy wasn't ready to give up. "Would the General reconsider if we demonstrated how much experience has taught us? As a personal expression of my appreciation I would be willing to advise my good friend, Addison Claywell, trust officer for the MacArthurs, on matters that would greatly enhance the family estate. Pro bono of course."

Capt. Drumond interrupted. "Lt. Murphy, General MacArthur sends you a special message: he wishes you to know that he wouldn't step aboard this ship even if it was in dry dock, nor would he trust you to handle his dollar-a-week Christmas Club savings account."

"His mistake," said Fabian.

The songs of Melos Crawford were becoming mournful and foreboding. Corporal Crawford, the third assistant engineer, had on-duty hours that kept him below deck. He wore earmuffs to protect the tympanic membrane of his inner ear from the high pitched screaming of the two max-speed GM diesel engines. Prior to having been selected to defend the Blue Ridge Mountains, Melos was acquiring some recognition among the locals of Monkey's Eyebrow, Kentucky, as a country-boy blue grass singer. When Army classification learned he was able to repair as well as tune his Gibson guitar, he was tagged as a mechanical expert and assigned to the 344 as a third-assistant engineer (known in the Navy as "oiler").

Off duty, folk singer Melos Crawford would take a three-legged stool up to the forecastle deck and, weather permitting, begin to play and sing those heart wrenching ballads about unrequited loves, neglected mothers, and simple homes that men longed to return to before some 4-F exemption ran off with their best girl. He had a strong voice, which carried fore and aft. The crew enjoyed his performances and there would be the occasioned tear when the lyrics described "that shanty back home that means more than a palace to me." Even hard-nosed Fabian Murphy found it difficult to look his usual skeptical self when Melos sang about the evils of gambling and deception. Two years earlier, it was Melos and his music that probably saved the ship and our lives when we were crossing the Gulf of Mexico. We had just delivered supplies to Fort Jefferson in the Dry Tortugas and were returning to New Orleans. Around one a.m. in Mid-Gulf, our sister ship, the FS214, was outbound for Tampa, because of the wartime blackout, the crew did not know they were on a collision course with the 344. According to Captain Clarence Hires of the 214, their lookout heard some sort of "bellowing" off the port bow. The officer on watch made an emergency change of course to starboard and the FS214 passed our stern with, fewer than five-hundred feet clearance. Melos Crawford never missed a note.

Then, the melodic sermons began to change. The lyrics, no longer plaintive, were sad with suggestions that we begin to make peace with our Maker. But the big bomb had been dropped and the war was over. It was a time to rejoice for the first time, the crew complained about Melos' singing and so Lt. Baldwin suggested we have a meeting with Melos. Perhaps there was a problem we could help him with, perhaps counseling from our morale officer, Fabian Murphy.

"Maybe he just found out his girlfriend back in the states is pregnant," said Fabian. "No problem there. I can line him up with some chicks who would make Betty Grable look like Stalin's sister-in-law. I can probably find a couple with money. Let's call him in and tell him the good news."

It wasn't that simple. Melos explained that his intended had had surgery in her late teens. Something to do with ovaries. No way could she be pregnant. "Don't be too sure," said morale officer Murphy. "I understand research medics are doing wild things these days. Just read that a Scandinavian sex team working with a girl they thought was a boy ended up with a litter of six kids. My advice is to keep track of that little girl at home."

"Let's get back to Melos and his change of music style," said Lt. Darrow. "Corporal, what has caused you to go from elation to depression just after we heard the good news that we're going home?"

"Maybe he's got one of those little island girls pregnant," said Fabian.

"No, no," said Melos," It's just that I've always been a worrier. I worried about things that never happen – like my car might be stolen, my hair could fall out, the paint on the north side of my house would peel."

"I was a worrier, too," said Lt. Ronald Cuthburt, Chief Engineer." I even worried about my wife running off with the milkman until I checked the size of the bill I pay his company every month and realized that the guy would never jeopardize a good thing like that."

Melos Crawford continued. "One day my buddies pointed out that I was foolish to torture myself this way because the things you worry about never happen. For a while, this made sense, so I stopped worrying until I woke up last week and wondered whether all the things that hadn't happened because I worried about them might descend on me because I had put them out of my mind. I'm a cautious guy. I'm playing it safe. I'm really worried."

Melos was getting hard to follow. His music had confused us, and now this. Lt. Darrow, in his best chaplain-like voice, said gently," Corporal, what's troubling you now? Who are you worried about?"

Melos Crawford, gospel singer, hesitated, looked about the room and said softly, "You, gentlemen."

This was not what we expected. Fabian was the first to respond.

"We appreciate your concern, Melos, but you needn't worry about us. All of us have jobs waiting and homes to return to. Don't give us another thought. Get back to your cheerful music."

"I'm not worried about what you will find at home," said Melos. "I'm worried about whether you will get any of us home at all."

"What are you talking about, Corporal Crawford? I said. "Do you know something we don't—renegade enemy subs, loose-cannon atomic bombs, uncharted mines? Tell us what you know, Melos."

He looked as if he would be more comfortable holding his guitar and singing a sad song about a coalmine disaster. He glanced at the five proud officers of the non-combative FS344. "I know you."

Monty Morgan finally came to life. "What are you talking about?" he shouted in his broad Boston accent that made him insufferable in an argument. He always said " i deer" instead of "idea" and "Iler" for this aunt's name which was really "Ila." "Your remarks sound insulting and I demand an explanation!"

Maybe he's heard about your navigation expertise," said Fabian.

Melos looked resigned to making the best of a confrontation he had neglected to worry about. "We made it across the Pacific with a convoy, but our ship managed to get lost the second day out," he began. "For the past two years we've never been beyond the sight of land, yet ended up in the

How to Stay Afloat Wearing Army Boots

wrong assigned anchorage three times. Our cargo-handling included confusing the yard-tackle with the stay-tackle and dropping a two-ton amphibious DUKW into 300 feet of water. It took a Navy salvage vessel to keep us from sinking when our engineer opened a seacock instead of the sanitary expulsion valve. And then the first mate tried to bring down an enemy plane and shot the signal mast off the Tiapa. There was the time…"

"We get your point, Melos, but what do you want us to do? Throw ourselves on the mercy of Neptune, go to confession Sunday?"

"No, sir," said Melos. "It's the trip home I'm worried about. Captain Drumond told us we are going alone, no convoy, just three thousand miles of open water."

Navigation officer Monty Morgan spoke up again. "You're over-reacting, Corporal. I was a member of the Long Island Coast Guard auxiliary for more than ten years. I can recite and identify every navigation aid in Sheepshead Bay. I am an expert in deciphering code flags and served as commander of the Martha's Vineyard Yacht Club for two terms. You are in good hands with this crew. We're seasoned now."

Fabian was looking glum. "Hope that doesn't mean pickled. Three thousand miles—that's probably as the crow flies—and we never have sailed in a straight line."

Lt. Cuthbert, Chief Engineer, excused himself from the meeting to check on a bearing that was feeling warm. "Got to watch everything. Engine is the heart of the ship," he said as he left to make certain the seacock was in a closed position.

The tenor of the meeting had changed. Momentarily, we forgot Melos Crawford and began to think about wills, next of kin, insurance, and other subjects more depressing than any of Melos' lyrics. We were beginning to feel like the bird being pushed from the nest.

I saw that Melos was uncomfortable, so I said "Thanks for your thoughts, Melos. You're dismissed now."

He stopped at the door, "Is there anything in particular you want me to do, skipper?"

"Yes," I said. "Worry about us."

Chapter Seventeen

Elwood Corbin, our vociferous but comprehension challenged lookout, announced the approach of Captain Drumond's launch on the port quarter. In a voice that carried well, Elwood embellish his call with an editorial that included, "And he is bringing aboard a shiny alarm clock fastened to a wooden box."

Captain Drumond glared at Lt. Monty Morgan. "I imagine that you, as navigation officer, also recognized this instrument as an alarm clock. I had sent Monty down to welcome the Captain. Monty now saw the opportunity to make brownie points by expounding his maritime knowledge and the finer points of advanced navigation. "Oh, no," he said, "that is a chronometer. A fine one, too, which we desperately need ever since Lt. Murphy jammed up our present one by spilling a pot of coffee over it while he was trying to decode a monetary market report he had received from that shady boiler-room bunch back in Boston. He denied it but we knew it was Fabian because no one else uses that much sugar in his coffee. Got into the swivels on the gimbals and fixed the chronometer at a thirty-seven degree angle. As you probably know, Captain, I am very familiar with this instrument. We have one mounted on a pedestal in the foyer of the Booth Bay Yacht Club. Very famous. It is the chronometer used by the great navigator, Ferdinand Magellan. Very helpful to me."

We had become accustomed to Captain Drumond's incredulous mien of incredulity whenever he visited our ship, but now his look of skepticism was almost threatening. Reminded me of the time he discovered Snuffy was raising pigeons in the foc'sle head. Snuffy claimed they were squab, dressed and sent to him by his mother. Sold them to the officers' mess on the Fillmore until someone discovered a GI-issued cigarette butt in one of the plumper birds.

"Lt. Morgan, you have been misled," began Drumond. "Magellan navigated the globe in 1504. The marine chronometer was devised in 1789. You'd better advise those sand-pounder day-sailors at the Yacht Club that they have been conned. Maybe Lt. Fabian Murphy sold them their vintage chronometer."

At the sound of his name Fabian joined us and inspected the new instrument with the eye of a professional. "Ah ha," he said, "this thing is more than six hours off. Needs adjusting already."

Captain Drumond displayed remarkable patience. "Not only hours, it is more than a day off," he said. "The chronometer is set on Greenwich time at the prime meridian. The difference between the setting on the chronometer and local time is longitude. Get it?"

"I'm basically a dead-reckoning man," said Monty Morgan. "I have sailed from Long Island sound to Bar Harbor and knew where I was every minute. No problem."

Drumond was not impressed. "Dead-reckoning is like visual flying. You are continuously in sight of something, a navigation light, a hunk of land, always something charted for a bearing. In two days you are going on a three-thousand mile voyage and the last thing you will see is this anchorage. You better dig out your Bowditch and start reading. You won't have the Fillmore to keep you from sailing over the edge."

Monty gulped. "What's Bowditch?"

"It's that four inch thick book you are using as a doorstop," said Fabian.

"Getting back to the chronometer," said Drumond, "every clock or watch has some error, forward or backward, usually seconds a day. Yours has been calibrated and a daily error rate determined. This rate must be applied for each day since the chronometer went into service. If a period goes by without the correction being made, you must multiply the number of days missed by the error rate to determine the correct Greenwich time. If this isn't done you'll never know your correct longitude."

Navigation officer Monty Morgan nodded. But, before he could reply Fabian Murphy broke in. "Captain Drumond, if Monty forgets any of this why couldn't he use the twenty-one Jewel Elgin I'm wearing to bring the chronometer up to date?

"It was a gift from an appreciative client who with my help doubled his net asset value. Never loses a minute. Wind it at the same time every day."

"Lt. Murphy, I am convinced that you don't know the difference between a turn buckle and a shoe horn. First, there is no way you can adjust a chronometer. It has been set to the time at the Prime Meridian when it was made. Your watch is set for local time, which only tells you when to hit the chow line. Stick to your morale-lifting duties, Lieutenant. This crew is going to need all confidence boosting it can get. Make sure their insurance papers are in order."

Captain Drumond handed to Monty Morgan a card with hand-printed lettering that stated the daily error rate of our chronometer. Also indicated was whether the correction was plus or minus/back or forward. "Don't lose this," warned Drumond. "Without it you won't know whether you are in the Philippine Sea or Pearl Harbor."

Navigation officer Morgan snapped to attention. "I will guard it with my life, sir. The most brutal of the enemy will never make me reveal this classified information so vital to our cause."

Captain Drumond sighed. "Just don't lose it, Monty."

We began to feel like the bird about to be kicked out of the nest. Second mate Baldwin said it was more like attending your own last rights. Even Captain Drumond, who never hesitated to let us know that real sailors were created by God, not by some Army-inspired act of Congress, began treating us with some compassion. "I am seeing that you are provisioned for 30 days at sea, even though you are scheduled to be in San Francisco no later than ten days from now. Remember, if you ever see the sun setting over the bow, turn around."

Snuffy called in his poker game receivables. One sailor from the Fillmore gave him a black book of San Francisco telephone numbers in lieu of an outstanding five dollars.

Raising the anchor was not exactly routine. I assigned our two Greek sailors this initial duty of getting underway. Pvt. Aristotle had the port anchor half way to the surface when Pvt. Mataxis missed the first rung on the foc'sle ladder and twisted his ankle while trying to reach the starboard windlass. Hearing Mataxis' shriek of pain, Aristotle ran to the aft rail to look down upon his writhing compatriot, forgetting to set the pawl on the windlass. The port anchor went crashing back to the bottom.

Lt. Darrows, observing the confusion, rushed forward and got the starboard windlass in operation, raising the anchor to the surface. Not realizing that the port anchor was back on the bottom, he signaled the bridge to move the ship ahead. Slowly underway, the stern began to swing out to the right while the bow became a pivot, turning gracefully about the embedded port anchor digging its flukes deeper in the muddy bottom.

Sailors on the other vessels had lined the rails to witness our departure. Some were cheering, particularly those who had bet we would never get underway. Self-consciously, we struggled with the reluctant port anchor for an hour before finally setting course.

Like a homing pigeon, Monty Morgan sailed east by north, using the Subic Bay light as his point of departure. Proudly, he took me to the chart room and pointed out our position, neatly X'd on the course line.

"How do you know this is right?" I said.

"No problem," said Monty. "The Subic Bay light has a range of sixteen miles. It just disappeared over the horizon, so voila', we are here—sixteen miles out."

This sounded too easy. "What do we do now?" I said. "We can't see the light anymore. What's the reference point from here on?"

Monty began to sound like a third-grade elementary teacher. "We know our speed—about fourteen knots. Every hour, we move our position on the course line ahead fifteen and one-half miles, and there we are, that much closer to home."

"What about the Japanese current? Isn't that supposed to take us north or some place we don't want to go?"

Navigation officer Morgan peered over the bridge wing. "I haven't noticed it yet," he said, "but when I do I will allow for it."

"You don't notice currents," I said. "I think you feel them. You'd better break out the sextant tomorrow and make some observations. Captain Drumond will be plenty annoyed if he wakes up tomorrow and finds us back at the anchorage. Remember what we were taught at that three-day navy school at Fort Eustis: 'Right red returning,' whatever that means – or was it 'add right deviation when correcting'? Anyway, do something besides making these chicken tracks on the chart. I want to know where we really are."

"You are over-reacting, skipper," said Monty. "Tomorrow at noon, just as the sun reaches its highest point in our meridian, I will check the new chronometer and we will have our exact longitude. I will yell 'mark' and you can record the time." He leaned back with the look of a satisfied Galileo.

"What about the chronometer error rate, do you still have it?" I said.

Monty smiled. "Look at this." Neatly engraved on the bulkhead just above the chart table was the chronometer error rate. "Always with us. No way to lose it. Used the chief's soldering iron and made it a part of the ship. A permanent record right where we use it. Good thing I did it. The card Drumond gave me fell out of my pocket and into the drink during that anchor-raising hassle yesterday. No problem—it's right here in front of us."

I had to agree it was a neat lettering job, but something seemed missing. Then I saw what wasn't there. "Monty, is that number plus or minus?"

Lt. Morgan looked puzzled. "What's the difference? It is the number that counts. Just apply it to the chronometer reading and you've got the correct Greenwich time."

I was beginning to feel like Captain Drumond. "Which way do you apply it—add or subtract? Forward or backwards? Small as that number is, it has to be multiplied by the number of days since it was set. That date is on the box. Do you remember whether there was a plus or minus sign on Drumond's card that you lost?"

"You know Drumond," Monty said, "always trying to be cute. I figure those marks on the card were his way of trying to confuse us. But, listen, why don't we do as Fabian suggested and use his twenty-one Jewel Elgin?"

Lt. Baldwin had been trying to bring the log up to date. "I am not recording this discussion," he said. "Someone might think I was writing script for stand-up comics. I will just mention that longitude doesn't interest us."

"Latitude is more important anyway," said Monty. "Tells us whether we are up or down. I will make a couple of celestial observations this evening and by morning we will know exactly where we are."

"Probably the Pacific Ocean," said Baldwin, putting his cherished stamp collection in a waterproof pouch.

"Day three—0800, we are lost." I was shocked to read Lt. Baldwin's log entry. "You can't say that," I said. "Logs are historic. They are read years later. Imagine someone twenty years from now writing a history of the war in the Pacific and discovering that this ship with you as first mate was 'lost' the third day out of harbor."

"What would you like me to say—'we have pinpointed our position to be exactly in the middle of the Pacific Ocean'?"

"Of course not, but we can be creative. You once wrote mail-order copy for a do-it-yourself pregnancy kit. Never worked, but you didn't go to jail. You were sincere without being self-incriminating."

Baldwin looked thoughtful. "We did move a lot of those kits until the FDA yanked them from the market. I got a letter from one lady who thought I should have contributed to the support of her twin girls. Never had a single complaint from the grow-new-hair ad, though."

"See what I mean?" I said. "It's better to know the questions than the answers. Let's try this for our log entry: 'Due to two days of sailing through the trailing edge of a typhoon, we are unable to activate the theodite with any degree of accuracy, resulting in a lapse rate indicating a state of weather equilibrium (Not a common condition in these latitudes). Irregular isobars have affected celestial observations to the extent that our lines of position are pulsating and preclude the possibility of a firm fix.' Now, isn't that better than 'we are lost'?"

Baldwin looked lost. "What's a theodite?"

"It doesn't matter. The field artillery captain who may be reading this two months from now won't know whether it's a sea anchor or a projector to show films about the perils of unprotected sex when on furlough.

Remember, Baldwin, the only thing more powerful than the truth is confusion." I was beginning to feel like a chaplain explaining the advantages of volunteering to go on a suicide mission.

Fabian Murphy entered the chart room, leading navigator Monty Morgan who appeared ready to part the Red Sea and free us from any doubt that we would ever find the Golden Gate of California. As advance man, Fabian announced that Monty had made a discovery that would determine our position and enable us to set a true course for the City by the Bay.

Lt. Morgan stepped forward, straightened his shoulders, and squinted over the tops of his GI-issue wire rims. The point of his bony nose quivered as he solemnly declared, "Gentlemen, we have just crossed the International Date Line."

There was silence until Lt. Darrow spoke up. "Damn it, now we've got to change our calendars. The cook thinks this is Friday and opened twenty-three cans of sardines for dinner. Wait until he finds out it is Thursday. Hope that fish will keep."

Fabian was skeptical. "How do you know?" Did you see a yellow line in the water? Maybe a can buoy with 'east' lettered on one side and 'west' on the other."

"Of course not," said Monty. "Just applied mathematics to determined we were one-hundred eighty degrees east of the prime meridian at Greenwich. I compared the time on the chronometer with Fabian's twenty-one jewel Elgin and the difference was twelve hours which told me we were on the International Date Line."

"Hold it, Monty. What about the error rate of the chronometer?" I said. "Didn't you tell me you didn't know whether it was plus or minus?"

Monty smiled. "I averaged it," he said. "I added the two possible corrections, plus and minus, and divided by two.

Believe it or not, it came out zero. Made everything easy. Now, we have a north-south line of position."

"Yeah, a line of position 1256 miles long," said Baldwin. "We could be either under the polar ice cap or off the coast of New Zealand. Monty, with your skills you could qualify as a backup navigator for Amelia Earhart."

"No problem," said Monty. "We just get an east-west line of position and there we are, at the intersection, with a fixed location on the chart. Smooth sailing from now on, Skipper."

"How long will it take to get that latitude position?" said Fabian. "Do you think we will still be afloat? You must have been a mathematics major to devise that plus and minus averaging method. Your Long Island commodore buddies will be green with envy when they hear about it."

Monty responded with equal sarcasm. "Your remarks indicate you will never be a Euclid. Applied math, to you, is acquiring a baby in one month by getting nine girls pregnant. Stick to your morale building, Lieutenant. I'll handle the navigation."

Two days later, Monty was still searching for a celestial fix that would show us on water. He confused Arcturus with Betelgeuse, which put the ship in the Indian Ocean. It was time to face up to it—we were lost again.

The signalman suggested we use the radio, although it was fixed frequency that would allow transmission only with the harbor division at Manila. Anywhere else would require message relay in both directions.

After contact, Fabian volunteered to be our spokesman and in his diplomatic manner work up to the subject of being lost. Initially, there was the usual radio chitchat with the duty officer until finally Fabian said, "Where are we?"

There was a moment of hesitation, then "You tell us."

The next morning, Elwood Corbin, our dedicated lookout, sighted a ship on the southeast horizon. It was a small Navy tanker on a westerly heading. Our crew was ecstatic. There was life, after all, east of the International Date Line. We changed course immediately and headed toward the tanker. Now we would have a point of reference from which to set a course to San Francisco. After thirty minutes, it became apparent we were not gaining on the tanker. It was faster and we were losing ground. Lt. Darrow, once again, found distress rockets in the life raft.

Baldwin was a little apprehensive about using them. He had been reading Knight's Modern Seamanship that stated that flares were to be used only when ships or personnel were in danger.

"We are in danger of being lost and never heard of again," said Fabian. "All we are going to do is ask for their position, and then get out of their hair. No sweat!"

It was settled. The flares were fired and through the binoculars we could see the tanker changing course and heading in our direction. We were saved.

Forty-five minutes later the tanker was within megaphone hailing. An officer in a neatly pressed Naval uniform stood on the bridge wing and asked if we were sinking or was there fire on board.

"No, no," I shouted, "We want directions. Where are we?"

There was a brief period of silence and then, "Repeat, please. Can't read you."

Monty Morgan took over. "We need to know your position so we can plot a course to San Francisco. We are sort of...lost." The two ships were drifting closer. So close that Snuffy at the stern was having a conversation with one of the tanker seaman leaning on the fantail rail. Megaphones were no longer necessary. The captain of the tanker stepped forward and shouted, "Are you telling me that you pulled us more than thirty-five miles off course and set back our ETA by four hours just to ask where you are?"

"Sort of like that, sir," said Monty. "It's a tradition of the sea. The New York yacht club encourages all its members to extend every courtesy to fellow sailors—particularly if they are lost."

It was apparent that the tanker captain was making every effort to control his emotions. Noticing Snuffy and one of his seamen fraternizing over the stern rails, he bellowed an order sending the man below, and implied that there was danger of picking up an Army virus that turned men's brains into mush. Directing his red-faced attention back to us, he said in a calm voice, "You want to know where you are? I'll tell you." Monty opened his notebook and poised his pencil. "You are precisely north of the equator and east of Japan." He shoved both controls of the telegraph to full forward, strode back into the pilothouse without a gestured of farewell, and left us to plot our new position.

"Better than nothing," said Fabian. "Now we know we are in the Northern Hemisphere. But that Japan bit, I'm not certain. With our in-house Henry the navigator we could be in the English Channel."

It was Snuffy who came forward with salvage value from our Naval encounter. During his conversation with the tanker seaman, he learned they were out of San Diego bound for the Marshall Islands. Leading us to the chart space, Snuffy took a straight edge and drew a line from San Diego to the Marshall's.

"There is your east-west position line," he said. "Now, we advance, Lt. Morgan's Date Line the distance we have sailed since crossing it and where it intersects with the tanker's course is our position."

There was period of respectful silence while we stared at Monty Morgan. "Very logical," he said. "I knew that when I determined we were crossing the International Date Line we were on our way to a fixed position." He looked around for some support.

Lt. Darrow was the first to respond. "Monty, if you had just majored at Harvard in something other than the sex life of flowers at high altitudes, Corporal. Snuffy would not have had to leave his rope-splicing duties to figure out where we are."

Fabian joined in. "I'm suspicious about the Date Line business—seems that we reached it awfully fast. Look at the chart. We must have been flying to cross it in less than two days—all the way from Manila. Maybe somebody moved it a few hundred miles west and Drumond forgot to tell us."

Navigator Morgan was defensive. "There was no way I could have struck up a conversation with the seaman on the tanker. You know military regs: officers cannot fraternize with enlisted men. Snuffy had the advantage."

Rockford Baldwin was still apprehensive about the future. "What about the Japanese current? They say it travels north and keeps Anchorage, Alaska, at a comfortable temperature. Do we wait until it begins to warm up on deck before getting concerned?"

"I will be alert for any indication of marine fluctuation which might affect our course, and, of course, make the proper adjustments," said Monty.

"What about now?" I said. "What's the next step that will get us home before the food runs out?"

"No problem Skipper," Monty assured me. "I'm plotting a course from our present position directly into San Francisco Bay. In a few days we will be on the wharf and eating oysters on the half shell."

"The first thing I am going to do is apply for a surplus WAC," said Fabian.

Something was wrong. Lt. Darrow was beginning his climb to the bridge deck to relieve Monty Morgan at the beginning of the morning watch when he noticed a beautiful sunrise over the stern taffrail. Admiring nature's way of announcing a new day, Darrow suddenly recalled that twelve hours earlier he had witnessed a colorful sunset sinking below the same after-section of the ship. Unless some influential person, like maybe Fabian Murphy, had changed the rotation of the earth, the ship was sailing due west! Bounding into the enclosed portion of the bridge, he tripped over the raised threshold and finished his entrance sprawled on his back at the feet of a smiling Monty Morgan.

"I admire your eagernous, Lieutenant," said Monty, "but you are four minutes ahead of your watch."

"No rush because I am in the middle of a course correction."

Scrambling to his feet and recovering his breath, Lt. Darrow blurted, "You turkey! We are heading west! What happened? Forgot your tooth brush?"

Not waiting for an explanation, Darrow grabbed the intercom and screamed in my ear, "Monty's gone Asiatic! He's got us on a two-hundred seventy degree heading. We will be back in Subic Bay before lunch!"

When I reached the bridge, Fabian and Baldwin had joined Darrow, eager to hear the theory of wrong-way navigation. "I can understand your apprehension, "began Monty in a condescending manner. "I realize that some of you are not acquainted with creative navigation. Last night I reviewed my computations in determining the International Date Line and discovered the correct time of crossing was thirty-six hours later than the time we had previously determined."

"Don't say 'we'," said Baldwin. "You were the impeccable authority who gave us the word."

Lt. Morgan continued. "After discovering the error I realized that our actual position must jibe with the log book. It was not difficult to figure out that by sailing a reciprocal course for one half hour we would be back in a position which would agree with the log book."

Monty looked about the space with the expression of a father who had just finished delivering a lecture to his four-year-old son on what every young man should know about sex.

Fabian was the first to speak. "Hey, Monty, why didn't you consider reversing the engines and backing up for half and hour? That way our compass course would be the same as when we were going forward. That should please Capt. Drumond if he lives long enough to check our log."

It was time for me to contribute something to this erudite discussion. "Why didn't you just correct the log book to agree with our real position? As navigating officer you have the authority to keep the log authentic."

"A matter of impression," said Monty. "Anyone reviewing our log and seeing position corrections would get the impression we were confused, don't you see?"

"Heavens, no," said Fabian. "Stupid, maybe, but never confused."

Lt. Morgan checked his watch. "Time," he announced. "Time to return to our former course." With a voice of command authority, he turned to the helmsman. "Private Hassen, bring the ship about to its original course and continue to hold so until changed by an officer of the watch."

Private Hassen looked confused. "Sir, what is the original course?

Navigator Morgan looked about the bridge for help, and then hesitantly said, "East."

"Wait a minute," said Lt. Baldwin. "There are one-hundred eighty degrees of east. East from here could be anywhere from Patagonia to the Beaufort Sea. Give the helmsman a firm course so at least we can draw a straight line on the chart. Looks professional, you know."

Monty's erect stature was beginning to melt back to its usual stoop. He produced a pocket notebook and began to compute, mumbling and grimacing as he compiled a page of numerals that looked like a racetrack tote sheet.

Finally, after several erasures and recapitulations that carried over to a second page, he snapped the book closed, walked over to Private Hassen at the wheel, pointed his skinny arm toward the sunrise and said, "That way."

"Lost again," said Fabian Murphy. "Hope our next of kin have been notified."

From forecastle deck we could hear the plaintive sound of Melos Crawford's guitar. "We're doomed," said Barry Darrow. "He's playing 'Nearer My God to Thee.' Now you have a real morale problem on your hands, Fabian."

"No sweat. I'll just give him those girlie magazines I brought aboard in Manila," said the personnel officer. "That will keep his mind off perdition until we reach Sin City in California."

On day twelve, Chief Engineer Ronald Cuthburt reported the ship was low on fresh water and from now on it would be saltwater showers for everyone.

Fabian was outraged. "When I volunteered to serve I was told I might be shot, captured or tortured, but I never agreed to salt water showers. I refuse to accept this marginally!"

"You never volunteered—you were drafted," I said. "You don't have to accept showers at all. When you become rancid we can always drag you on the end of the taftrail log line. Of course, you might look like shark bait and we would have to keep an eye on you. Hate to lose part of that log line. Army would probably charge me for it. Irresponsible use of government property."

Before Fabian could respond, the intercom whistle from the engine room began to shriek. Chief Engineer Cuthburt was yelling.

"What are you Tidal Basin commodores doing up there! There's mud coming through the cooling water system! We're sucking up the bottom! I am shutting down the engines before we grind them into steel wool!"

This was alarming, but not to Monty Morgan. "There you are," he said. "That means we are getting close to land. I have brought you across the Pacific like a homing pigeon. Told you my Narragansett Bay dead reckoning system was infallible." He flashed his toothy smile, looking like an underfed Gandhi.

"Are you for real?" I shouted back. "Your system may be more dead than reckoning! Mud in the cooling water means we are about six inches from the bottom and heading toward shoal water. That pigeon you resemble may never see home!"

Undaunted, Monty stepped into the chartroom and entered in the log: "Lt. Montgomery Morgan, Navigator, at 1430 hours, reports landfall."

Lt. Baldwin looked at the entry and added, "under the keel."

Without power, we dropped an anchor to keep from drifting closer to shallow water and waited for the tide to lift the ship the two feet the tide-table predicted, if Lt. Darrow had read it correctly.

At 1945 hour, just after sundown, Lt. Cuthburt reported the cooling water was running clear and that he was restarting the engines. We ran in an outward direction until the lead line showed five fathoms of water. The question now was where do we go from here.

Fabian suggested we scan the horizon for a glow in the sky. "San Francisco is loaded with night spots all flashing lights like crazy. My favorite has a giant figure of a stripper completely outlined in orange neon. Attracts more attention than the Washington Monument. That alone could be a real navigational aid."

"That was prewar," said Baldwin. "War Department hasn't lifted the blackout yet. I am afraid we will have to take desperate measures and rely on our own Vasco da Gama, Montgomery Morgan, the Third."

Always ready for center stage, Monty stepped forward to announce that he would be measuring the angle of the moon above the horizon and plotting a course directly into San Francisco Bay. Turning to Fabian, he said, "And you, Lt. Murphy, in a few hours, can be frequenting those waterfront dives and practicing the wanton carnality for which you are noted."

"If you mean great sex, I am all for it," said Fabian, "but we of the enlightened class prefer to call it pollinating the species. But don't get my hopes up. If I have to wait until you get those moon measurements figured out I may be just a consultant in matters of *l'amore*."

Before Lt. Morgan could move out to the bridge wing to begin his observation, there was a cry from the focsle deck. It was Elwood Corbin, lookout, announcing the first reportable thing he had seen in six days. It was a dramatic moment for him while we wondered whether Elwood had spotted another sperm whale or someone had tossed Melos Crawford's guitar overboard. It was tantalizing to watch Elwood draw himself up to his full five-foot-six inch height and in his varying pitch voice report what he was seeing: "Two points abaft the port beam, a flashing light of intermittent intensity at the horizon line."

Elwood must have been reading his Modern Seamanship Manual. We were not sure where two points abaft the beam was, but we rushed to the port side, and there it was, a barely discernible navigation light that seemed to disappear as we bobbed up and down. Now we knew how Columbus felt when he first spotted those beach barbecues on the San Salvador beaches.

Monty was ecstatic. "There it is, just as I planned it! In a few hours we will be drinking martinis at the OC on Treasure Island, if the Navy lets us in with our scrubby Army uniforms."

"Cool it, Monty," said Darrow. "We are a long ways from that light. With our luck they could blow a fuse and we would be lost again. Better keep measuring that moon."

Lt. Baldwin had been studying the light through the binoculars, trying to identify it. "Two short flashes and a long," he announced. "I will try to find it in our Coastal Navigation Aids publication so we can plot it." Monty set a course for the light and then retired to his cabin to bring his diary up to date and modestly record the part he played in bring the FS344 and its crew safely home.

Lt. Baldwin returned to the chart room, puzzled and exasperated. "Like everything else on this ship the Navigation Aids book is obsolete. Why didn't Drumond see that we had a current copy of this publication?
Believe it or not, our book identifies the beacon we're looking at as the Cape Flatterly light. Hell, Cape Flattery is somewhere near Canada."

"Doesn't matter," said Darrow. "We know where we are. Soon as we find out where the Navy wants us to park we will be ready for shore leave."

It was chilly and misty about 0815 when we came abeam the light we had been chasing for the past four hours. The water was cold and dark, which indicated plenty of depth even for aircraft carriers. Out of the fog we saw a pilot boat approaching us. A doughty figure was standing at the bow. He was wearing a single-breasted Naval uniform with a vest that carried a gold pocket watch and fob across his ample girth. Incredibly, instead of the traditional Naval officer's visored headpiece, he wore a brown felt fodora.

As the pilot boat came alongside, he scrambled up our Jacob's ladder like a person who had been boarding ships since the days of Admiral Dewey. With a no-nonsense stride he was in the pilothouse in seconds and giving orders to the helmsman.

For a moment I thought we were being boarded by the Mafia, until he turned to me and said, "I am your pilot, Kevin Dockerdy, assigned to take you into the sound. This monkey suit I'm wearing must have surprised you, just like it embarrasses me. Damn government. When the war began all pilots were put under the direction of the Navy. First thing they did was make us wear Naval officer uniforms. Makes us look like bus drivers. I had mine made special. Notice, single breast jacket with a vest. Place to carry my watch. Nothing in their directive mentioned a hat, so I wear a respectable pilot's felt fedora. They don't pay us but tell us how to dress. Our checks come from the Maritime Division."

When Mr. Dockerdy finally stopped speaking to take a breath, I broke in, "We don't need a pilot. We have just come across the Pacific and we can certainly find out way to our berth."

Pilot Dockerdy smiled. "That's what they all say. Without a pilot you wouldn't get half way through Wrangle Narrows without being hung up on Ripple Rock. It's about four feet under the surface and rips a hull from stem to stern. Besides, it is a government reg. No ship comes beyond Port Townsend without a pilot."

"Where is Wrangle Narrows?" said Monty Morgan. "Don't seem to find it on my chart."

"You must have really old charts," said Pilot Dockerdy. "Wrangle Narrows has been here since the dinosaurs. Let me take a look."

Monty brought out the chart and said with some pride, "Notice how our course hit the Bay dead center."

Kevin Dockerdy stared at it, then at Monty and me. "Gentlemen," he began softly, "where do you think you are?"

"According to my calculations," said Monty, "we are in the Gulf of Faralones just abeam the Golden Gate light and entering San Francisco Bay. Pin point navigation."

"Pretty wide pin," said our feisty pilot. "Right now you are nine-hundred and twenty miles off course, moving past the Cape Flattery light in the middle of the Juan de Fuca Strait. At this speed you should be at pier forty-four in Seattle in about ninety minutes. Play your cards and someone might invite you to the top of the Mark Hopkins for a drink."

"Damn Japanese current," said Monty Morgan. "Never could trust those Orientals."

"I wondered what had happened to The Bridge," said morale officer Fabian Murphy.

How to Stay Afloat Wearing Army Boots

Chapter Eighteen

It was fortunate that pilot Kevin Dockerty's distain for the Navy and all things related to the descendants of John Paul Jones provided for him an empathy with a crew of embarrassed soldiers that had just wandered almost nine-hundred miles off course. He was almost benevolent.

"Sod–busters like you guys are bound to have a few problems. That close–order drill training you've had makes you look gung – ho parading up and down the pier, but underway, 'twin screw' to you probably means a pair of hooker stowaways. It's those sixty–day Navy wonders that bothers me. Those swabbies are supposed to be professional, but unless there are fifty fathoms under their keel they are in trouble. And I am supposed to be working for them wearing this bellhop outfit. Next month the uniform goes to Good Will. I am keeping the vest, though."

"What's the next step asked?" said Fabian. "Are you taking us into Seattle? I've got a couple of telephone numbers I would like to exercise in that area—you know, friendly recreation for the weary."

Dockerty smiled. "I know what you mean, young fella, but we can offer some very pleasant hospitality right here at Port Angeles. Seattle is sixty miles down the Sound.

The Navy in that town would probably put you on exhibit and charge admission to see the crew that couldn't sail straight."

"I thought we might have to go into Seattle to top our tanks," I said. "We are low on fuel and almost out of food and water."

"No problem," said pilot Dockerty. "You can refuel right here at the Frisco Docks and get your provisions from Fort Worden at Port Townsend. You are going to have enough explaining to do when you finally get to San Francisco without justifying sixty more miles off course just so the smiling Irishman here could make a couple of phone calls."

Fabian was still interested in recreation, not necessarily the YMCA. "Understand that you are out here in the straits three weeks at a stretch. Must get lonesome jockeying wayward ships along an uninhabited coast, passing those vibrant centers of civilization like Port Renfrew, River Jordon, and Sooke. I haven't seen a female since we entered the straits. The chiefs here must be keeping the squaws confined to the tepees."

Pilot Dockerty winked. "We're not as deprived as you seemed to think we are."

"I know you are home only once a month," said Fabian. "You are probably the waterway cribbage champion who whoops it up on Saturday night with the other pilots throwing darts at each other."

Kevin Dockerty continued to smile. "You may be interested to know that just outside Port Angeles we have an area affectionately known as 'Ecstasy Acres.' Nice little subdivision inhabited by some very hospitable ladies. A few of the unattached might even be amused by a rough-edged would-be sailor like you."

Fabian brightened. "You rascal you," he said. Now I know why you can't play cribbage worth a damn. Tell me more about 'Ecstasy Acres'." He looked at Dockerty with new respect.

"Nothing much about it," said the pilot. "A few small, neat cottages not far from the end of the bus line." He hesitated a moment. "I rent one of the cottages. Just a small one-bedroom with a decent view. I have a full-time housekeeper, a pleasant young Philippine Myomassologist."

"My God!" said Lt. Baldwin. "A revolutionary!"

"No, no," said Dockerty. "A back rubber. She massages my back. A welcome relief after standing on the cold bridge of a tramp steamer for nine hours. A wonderful arrangement, worth every cent of the rent I pay. A very loyal and appreciative lady."

"Where did you say Ecstasy Acres is?" Fabian began wiping the dust from his shoes.

Observing pilot Kevin Dockerty handle a ship was like watching a virtuoso coax heavenly music from a second-rate violin. He was a third-generation pilot and remembered when he was twelve accompanying his father on ships entering Puget Sound. Aircraft carriers of deep draft heading for Bremerton were his specialty, guiding them through the maze of islands that filled the sound from Port Townsend to Tacoma. In one-hundred fifty years no Dockerty had ever laid a ship on a rock, he told us. "When that happens, it's over. We will climb down the Jacob's ladder for the last time and start selling life insurance or vacuums."

It was dark when Dockerty took over the bridge and began to conn our ship through the Juan de Fuca Strait. Standing in the pilot area with his back against the bulkhead and holding the required cup of Black coffee, he appeared to be seeing nothing. Then, quietly to the helmsman, "Come right one quarter rudder and hold."

According to maritime law the captain is always responsible for a ship's safety and is expected to over-ride a pilot if there is any sign of danger. But who would have the courage to revoke pilot Dockerty's orders? The ship was slowly swinging to the right. When would he stop it? The famous Ripple Rock was off our starboard. Would the swinging stop before we were on it? Had Dockerty gone to sleep? Then, from the back of the pilothouse, "Steady as she goes."

"Steady as it goes," said the helmsman as he returned the rudder indicator to amidship. The ship glided by the rock that had been taking the bottom out of ships ever since the Russians began bringing their furs into Seattle.

Dockerty never looked at the compass, never touched the wheel or the telegraph. I kept running from one bridge end to the other to watch the shoal water and rocky ledges sliding by on both sides. Rogue currents and the force of an ebbing tide made holding a steady helm difficult. At one point the bow fell off to the left and it seemed that we would be helplessly broadside to the current. A couple of barely audible orders from Dockerty brought us back to a steady up–stream heading. After a two–hour nail–biting run, during which Dockerty never left his lanquid position against the bulkhead, I heard him give his final command: "Finished with engines." Looking over the bridge rail I realized we lay quietly alongside the pier. It was an accomplishment in docking that would have taken me most of the day just to come along side without wiping out a cluster of piling.

After making certain we were secure, Dockerty came over to me. "Word about you showing up here at Seattle has reached the Army base in San Francisco. The CO down there is a Colonel Wilfred Margin. Madder than a hooked tarpon. Says you caused him to fall overboard in the Gulf of Mexico. Surprised that you're not in Anchorage, Alaska."

"There goes my retired reserve officer pension," I said. "Margin will probably want me to face a general court. Probably charge me with trying to steal an Army vessel."

Dockerty now flashed his trade–mark wink. "I've got an out for you." He reached into the ever- present valise that contained his razor, toothpaste, and a framed photo of his wife and two children. He extracted a box of what appeared to be fifty small flat wafers. "Batteries," he said. "When you get to

San Francisco, start screaming about being sent to sea with defective equipment that endangered the ship and the lives of your crew. Point out that pilot Kevin Dockerty had discovered you were sailing with a compass with twenty degrees of uncompensated left deviation, pulling you to the north, far off your intended course. Threaten to go to the DOD at the Pentagon. That will shake them."

"But there is no deviation we don't know about," I said.

"Ah, ha, there will be." Dockerty spread the wafers across the chart table. "Brand new. Just developed for fancy watches and hearing aids. We tape all fifty of them on the right side of the binnacle post. They will repel the card toward the west and you will be sailing twenty degrees off course. A very dangerous situation. It works. I've tried it."

"But what happens when they spot it?" I said.

"They won't. Not the way I will install them. We will use electrician's tape on both sides of the binnale post. Make it look decorative. Remember, some Army inspectors think a compass is something used to make circles on a piece of paper."

"What about experts? They will bring in people who catch on fast."

"Sure they will," said the pilot. "They will call in a Navy degaussing team. These guys are good. They can detect a fruit fly on a compass rose at forty feet. But before they come aboard you will have removed the batteries and tossed them over the side. In contrast to the Army team, they will find nothing wrong with compass. Their report will imply that the Army inspectors should clean their bifocals and stick to semaphore code work. Smelling the possibility of ridicule involving Marine professionalism, Transportation HQ will probably drop the entire matter and raise hell with you about your crew being out of uniform while swabbing the decks."

"You should have been in pictures," I said.

Reprovisioned and ready to sail, we were set to leave Port Angeles the next day at 0600. That night Fabian requested shore leave with relaxation and "recreation" in mind. Before daybreak a taxicab drove on to the pier and Fabian came aboard without his shoes. Reluctant to talk about it, he finally explained that the situation had been caused by a broad who couldn't keep track of the calendar. When he rang her doorbell and explained that due to war fatigue and hand-to-hand combat he suffered short term memory loss and needed directions to return to his base, she invited him in for tea, cookies, and counseling. She said her keeper would not be back until Wednesday. "About two in the morning I heard keys rattling at the front door. 'Are you sure he said Wednesday? This is only Tuesday.' She was puzzled, too, and then said, 'Oh my God! I've been using last year's calendar!' I could hear someone coming down the hall and decided it was time use the window. I was lucky to get my pants on before he was rattling the bedroom doorknob. It was then I decided to hell with the shoes."

"Sounds like you were visiting Ecstasy Acres last night," I said.

Promptly at 0600, before daylight, pilot Kevin Dockerty came aboard ready to shepherd us to the sea buoy and send us on our way to the City on the Bay. Something was wrong. Instead of his usual genial self he was red – faced and sputtering.

"Somebody has been sleeping with my mistress!" He gave a threatening look at the entire crew.

Fabian was the first to respond. "Any idea who it was?"

"Not yet," thundered Dockerty, "but when I do he will wish he had been born a vestal virgin. We'll be taking a ride together out to the sea buoy. I'll be coming back alone. The foredeck on those pilot boats can get pretty slippery on choppy days. Very easy to slide off, happens regularly."

Fabian gulped. "How can you identify him? Did you see him?"

Dockerty reached into the brown paper bag he was carrying and pulled out a pair of neatly polished shoes. "The snake took off so fast he left his shoes. Soon as I find their owner our pilots' association will apply a bit of maritime discipline. It won't be pleasant. Who'd he think was paying the rent for that pad?"

Fabian took the shoes. "Maybe I can help." Like a professional cobbler he reached down into the toe area, scrutinized the sole, and sniffed the leather." Looking up at Dockerty, he declared with the air of a magistrate, "Just as I thought. These are Government Issue US Navy, off–duty oxfords."

"I knew it!" said Dockerty. "I knew the scum–bag Navy would be involved in this violation of personal rights! By the way, doesn't the Navy wear black shoes? These are tan."

"Not with their summer khaki uniforms," said Fabian. "Your man was dressed to kill, wearing an off–duty coordinated uniform with shoes to match."

Returning the shoes to his bag, Dockerty resumed his authority as our pilot. "Shorten up the bow lines and let's move out," he said. "Got to get you guys headed in the right direction. Don't want you to end up in Anchorage."

Ninety minutes later we were rounding the sea buoy and on a southerly heading. As Kevin Dockerty clambered down the ladder into the pilot boat, he looked up at the group of us at the rail and said, "Thanks for your help, Fabian."

We were on our way again. Pilot Dockerdy left us at the sea buoy to move aboard an incoming troop transport which would be under his command until it docked at pier 14 in downtown Seattle. As he clambered down the ladder into the pilot boat, his parting instructions were, "Head in a southerly direction all the way, and don't forget there are 20 degrees of built-in deviation with those hearing aid batteries.

And you, navigator Morgan, remember when uncorrecting, going from a true course to a compass heading, you add westerly deviation. Got it?"

Monty Morgan nodded and in the tone of a Fletcher Christian, responded, "Like crossing Oyster Bay on a short reach and correcting for an off-shore blow. No problem." He scratched a couple of indecipherable equations in his notebook, snapped it shut and slipped it into his shirt pocket. His look of smug complacency left us feeling uneasy.

"Those were my best shoes," complained Fabian. "Now, that little boat-jockey will be wearing them every third Sunday at church showing off his sartorial good taste in footwear."

"Since when did the Navy start wearing tan shoes?" I said. "That was one of your 'tell them what they want to hear' lines, wasn't it?"

"Sure, but Dockerdy was so determined to pin the blame for this innocent assignation on the Navy that he would believe anything that implicated anybody wearing a sailor suit."

Lt. Baldwin was interested. His shore leave was a bust. He had met two girls at the USO and when he asked the blonde with the tapered legs if she would like to split off and go somewhere alone with him, she said sure and took him down the street to the Methodist Church where they joined a Bible study group backed up with oatmeal cookies and ice cream. It was not an earth-shaking evening. Before returning to his ship he made certain that the other soldiers wandering about the town saw him visiting the GI pro-station. No one was going to think he batted zero.

"How about Dockerdy's Philippine live-in?" he said to Fabian. "Was she as fabulous as he claimed?"

"A sensational back-rubber," said Fabian. "Relaxed me so much I went to sleep and didn't wake up until I heard the master of the house coming home. Great night out but not worth losing a pair of Johnson & Murphy shoes. Next time

I'll wear the Government Issue ones. Claim I lost them in action. Expendable items in wartime."

It was good to be back in command of our own ship again, heading down the coast to its final berth in San Francisco where the crew claimed they had left their heart, or at least a hot phone number. Good until the second morning when Lt. Darrow came on watch and reported there was nothing to be seen—not a lighthouse, a channel marker or range light. Just water on all sides.

Pilot Dockerdy had warned us to avoid sailing so close to the coast that we could see land. "Just close enough to pick up navigation aids showing above the horizon. If you see land, you are too close and will probably get hung on a mud flat or, worse, a rock with the propeller spinning out of control like a mix-master. Pretty embarrassing, even for the Army," he warned.

Now it appeared we were being overly cautious. There was nothing to see. Elwood Corbin, our devoted-to-duty lookout, was beginning to complain he had nothing to report, not even a seagull or unwanted jetsam. Nothing but cold choppy water on all sides.

Navigator Monty Morgan had a ready explanation: "The coast, right about here, makes a big indentation. We are sailing due south, so at this point we are farther out to sea. At the next bump in the coastline we will be back in sight of the USA."

Lt. Darrow had been peering at the compass. "Bumps aside, have you been applying Dockerdy's correction factor for the deviation caused by those batteries strapped to the binnacle?"

"Of course," snapped Monty. "Even you remember the formula: 'when correcting, subtract westerly deviation.' "

"But you are 'uncorrecting'," protested Darrow. "You are going from true course to compass – that's uncorrecting. You should be adding!"

"Don't try to confuse me," said the navigator. "I know what I am doing."

"Whatever you are doing is taking us back to sea," I said. "Keep this up and we will be at Pearl Harbor by Wednesday. Swing this ship around and head due east until we see something that reminds us of the United States."

Monty Morgan groaned. "The governing board of the New York Yacht Club would never sanction hit and miss navigation like this."

"Maybe they are not familiar with your 'bump' method of dead reckoning," said Darrow. "You applied the correction wrong and we have been sailing forty-five degrees off course for the last two hours. At this rate it is going to take us as long to get from Seattle to San Francisco as it did to cross the Pacific."

For three hours we ran directly toward the coast, with Monty shaking his head and grumbling about imprecise navigation. Around 2030 hours we raised the top of the cape lookout light on the Oregon Coast. Three hundred miles in two and a half days. Not an impressive record for the pride of the Transportation Corp water division. As the ship changed to a southerly course, Elwood Corbin was pleased to announce that a Coast Guard cutter was approaching from two points off the port quarter. We assumed that meant somewhere ahead on the left side. A signal requested permission to come aboard. To avoid running over the Coast Guard patrol boat engineer Cuthburt shut both engines down and we bobbed around while the trim young Navy ensign brought his vessel skillfully alongside and leaped aboard.

He explained that the Coast Guard had been alerted to watch for us and make certain we were on a course that would bring us within waving distance of California. Most welcomed was the sack of mail he brought. Among Fabian's was a demand by a Boston District Court that he settles immediately an award made to the West End Mothers Investment Club in the amount of six-thousand four-hundred dollars, for selling misinformation "bordering on defraudation." Fabian said it was a misunderstanding, resealed the envelope, and marked it "undeliverable."

Chapter Nineteen

Lt. Baldwin was upset when his mother in her letter wanted to know what medals he had been awarded so she could include them in the servicemen's honor section of the Akron Beacon Journal.

"Do you realize," he shouted, "that the only awards we have is the Good Conduct Medal and the Pacific Theater Ribbon—after all we have been through! What will our families think when we come marching home with a two-inch ribbon bar on our blouse? Somebody will make snide remarks like, 'was it tough duty handing out Hershey Bars with the Salvation Army?' We deserve recognition."

"You might get the Purple Heart if we could get Monty Morgan to shoot your leg off," said Fabian. "Beautiful ribbon and medal. Imagine the impression you would make, hobbling down the gangway, ribbons flapping in the breeze. Mayor would probably want to name the new comfort station after you. Monty would probably do the job, too. He never has liked you since he found out your grandfather came through Ellis Island. The Morgan family motto has always been 'America for Americans.' He hates those upstarts who come in the back door. I'll ask him."

"Now you are being your usual ridiculous self," said Baldwin. "I am serious about this. If we don't get some recognition people will get the impression we are noncombatant free loaders."

"So what's new?" said Fabian. "But, hey, talk to Snuffy. He has had more metals taken from him than the Lost Battalion ever won. He probably knows all the angles in convincing the Department of Defense that some glory-seeker deserves a medal."

"Good thought," said Baldwin. "Time is running short. War will be officially over and no one will remember us if we don't act fast. Snuffy may be a scoundrel to the Army but he is certainly a handy guardhouse lawyer for those of us who never completed officer orientation. I will talk to him today."

Monty Morgan's package included a hand-knit five-foot Shetland wool scarf from his intended bride, Sylvia Raginfield, the cream of Westchester society who waited patiently for him to return from the wars and claim her as well as the Morgan estate. A portrait painter was on hold, ready to preserve Monty's likeness on canvas to hang in the great room along side the other Morgan heroes who had fought so valiantly to preserve capitalism for America.

Always ready with advice, Fabian warned Monty not to speak during the sittings. "The artist might not appreciate those syllabic sprays you are so noted for. Remember, oil and water don't mix."

Lt. Darrow was not inspired by his mail from home: three money belts, a waterproof pocket Bible, and five sets of khaki underwear. "This makes nine money belts," he said. "Where does the home front think we get all this money that has to be protected? And all this khaki stuff. Army issue underwear is white. I have thirty-five khaki handkerchiefs and four khaki pajamas. Now that the war is over, I will be going home with a complete khaki wardrobe, from socks to earmuffs. May be I can get a job with the park rangers."

Snuffy's only package was from his father: a gross of Trojan contraceptives, with a simple message: "Enjoy." "Better than a money belt," said the corporal.

At Lt. Baldwin's urging we met with Snuffy in the wardroom to discuss ways of convincing the War Department that we deserved recognition of our devotion to duty during the past three years. Our legal advisor scowled as he stowed a pinch of snuff back of his upper lip. "Won't be easy," he said. "Considering the only ship we ever sank was one of our own and the DOD is threatening to bill us for the government property we've lost and there is a chance we will all be reduced in rank."

"There have to be some good things we did," said Fabian. "Like when we hauled all that Listerine and corn flakes to the men on the Gilbert Island, and the time we kept Capt. Drumond from stepping into the drink when private Aristotle cast off the painter on his launch before the good captain was aboard."

Snuffy was not encouraging. "Problem is, someone, not one of us, has to recommend the decoration. Capt. Drumond would go into hysterics if we asked him." Then he brightened, "There is a way— a Unit Citation!"

Baldwin was on his feet. "That's it!" he exclaimed. "I've seen those ribbons, nice green color. Would look great with my dress blouse. What's the next step? How do we get it before peace is declared and some desk general puts a moratorium on medals?"

Snuffy spoke softly, like a nursery school monitor explaining how to create a Mother's day card. "First, the Captain sends a communication to the War Department extolling the performance of the crew under hazardous conditions, and displaying service above self at all times without regard for personal safety or discomfort. Performance in carrying out the orders of their officers was exemplary and resulted in the successful accomplishment of an assigned mission in hostile waters."

"Is this our crew you are talking about?" said Monty Morgan.

"Doesn't matter," said Snuffy. "All citations sound pretty much the same. Just change a few key words. In summation, the skipper will recommend recognition of this valiant service and suggest that a unit citation would be an appropriate award from a grateful nation."

Lt. Darrow was dubious. "What about us?" Your eulogy doesn't mention the officers. How about when Monty got us lost three times? We are lucky to be returning in one piece."

Snuffy smiled. "That's the good part of the unit citation. Because you are compassionate, unselfish men, you want the credit to go where it is due - - to the seldom-recognized enlisted men in the crew. That is why you are recommending this citation."

"So what's in it for us?" said Fabian.

"Just this," said Snuffy. "A unit citation means everybody. Everybody from the cook to captain will be awarded the medal. It is a wonderful way for a CO to add to the fruit salad on his chest. Of course he has to take about 40 other people along but that's all right, it may be their only decoration."

"Let's go!" cried Baldwin. "Skipper, you have got to act fast. This show is coming to the final curtain and after that it will be 'what war?'"

As the commanding officer of sixteen men, I suddenly became the designated hitter in the matter of requesting deserved recognition for a crew that had so valiantly served their country—all to get Baldwin a medal to show his Mother's bridge club. In good executive fashion, I delegated the matter to a most capable subordinate, Snuffy.

"Get on this fast," I ordered. "Ensign Dale Franklin of the Coast Guard is still aboard eating the ice cream we picked up at Port Townsend. If we can keep him here for another half hour, we will ask him to take our official commendation request ashore and start it up the chain of command."

Lt. Monty Morgan was not impressed. "Do you mean that we officers will be getting the same ribbon as the enlisted men? There should be some distinction. After all, any outstanding performance was under our direction. I will wear mine only in parades, never at the Newport Commodore's Ball."

"You will be lucky if you are not wearing shackles," said Fabian. "When those clubhouse admiral buddies of yours find out your dead reckoning method had us lost most of the time, you may be reduced to dock jockey during presidential regattas."

"Lace-curtain shanty Irish," muttered Monty. "Sons of the steerage class, the cultured man's burden."

Within forty minutes Snuffy produced a formal unit citation recommendation, ready for my signature. Ensign Franklin had finished his second bowl of ice cream and was ready to cast off, promising to send our formal message through proper channels to the War Department. "You won't have to worry about getting to San Francisco," he assured us. "Every coast guard station along the California coast has been alerted to watch for you and make certain you're still on a southerly heading. Seem that this ship has a reputation for reciprocal headings."

I watched with envy as Ensign Franklin maneuvered the cutter away from our side. "Just a smart-ass kid," said Monty.

"Yeah, but with smarts like that on this ship there would be a few more piers still intact," I said.

Although it took another week, the trip down coast was uneventful. Every coast guard station we passed sent out a picket boat to make certain we were still heading in the general direction of the Golden Gate. Darrow said he was beginning to feel like a lost duckling with an anxious mother. Fabian wanted to stop over at Eureka to look up a "wild chick" he once knew. Lt. Cuthbert, chief engineer, tried to accommodate him by creating a fake break down, but an alerted second assistant detected the ploy and kept things running until we were well past the land of temptation.

It was Elwood Corbin, dedicated lookout, who first sighted the Golden Gate Bridge. His announcement was so elaborate it seemed that we might sail passed our goal before we knew what he was describing. Everyone was jubilant, particularly Fabian who was polishing the brass on his dress uniform and reviewing his list of "West Coast Encounters I Have Known."

Snuffy warned that because of our past trespasses we might all be confined to the ship until things had been sorted out. "Not the officers," said Fabian. "A few EM's will be required to stay aboard for security reasons and the officers will be ashore for debriefing by port authorities." Fabian regretted not having his J & M tan oxfords to impress his Frisco fans.

As we passed under the Golden Gate Bridge, two small Harbor Craft tugs came out to escort us and maneuver the ship to a vacant mooring at an Army coal dock. It was not the welcome we had expected. Just a couple of agricultural officers who demanded to know if we were bringing in any taboo plants or fruit. The more officious of the two gave the impression of examining a shipload of bubonic plague victims.

"Hope there are no lice aboard," he said. "If there are any I will have to quarantine the ship until the decontamination team gets down here. May take a week or ten days."

"You don't have any VD aboard, do you?" said the shorter of the two inspectors. "Last month we had a ship come in with three cases of syphilis. What a mess. The medics wanted to play it safe so they made the entire crew undergo the treatment program. Boy, were they pissed off. Imagine being five-hundred yards from Fisherman's Wharf and confined to ship for thirty days."

Our inquisitors informed us we were free to come ashore without fear of endangering the California avocado crop. Fabian appeared on deck looking as clean cut as a Hollywood celebrity on a recruiting poster. As he reached the gangway, he said, to me, "Lt. Murphy requesting permission to leave the ship for a little quail hunting." Without waiting for a reply, he turned and almost knocked over a messenger coming aboard with a communication from Col. Wilfred Margin, west coast water division commander, previously our Florida nemesis ever since he almost drowned after falling overboard during an inspection of our ship at Carrabelle, Florida. We always felt that he blamed us for his misstep and that he looked forward to a time when he could apply retributive justice.

"Hold fast," I said to Fabian. "This could include you." It did.

The message was fierce and to the point: "There is the implication that the crew of the FS344 is being considered for a Unit Citation. This headquarters feels that the recognition of devotion to duty brings honor to the entire water division and that it is appropriate to express our appreciation with some gesture of command reward.

"Therefore, it is my decision that the entire enlisted crew of the FS344 will be granted shore leave the first night the ship is in port, and that the officers will remain on duty for security purposes."

"There goes Murphy's Night at the Opera," said Lt. Darrow. "It's your fault, Fabian. If you hadn't shacked up with Monya, the Colonel's secretary, while he was sleeping off his hang-over aboard our ship, we wouldn't be stuck with duty tonight."

Fabian began to make loud piercing noises. "This is an outrage! It's a depredation of my rights as an officer and gentlemen! He can't get away with this! I've got friends! I will write my congressman and have that home guard colonel busted back to mess sergeant within a week! I am going ashore right now and you can tell Wilfred Margin I am bringing charges of inhumane treatment!"

It was time to apply pragmatic therapy. "If you leave this ship I will be obliged to report that you have disobeyed a direct order," I said. "You know that's a serious charge that could bring you ten years of confinement."

"Yeah, and Alcatraz is less than a mile away across the Bay. Mightily handy for the Army," said Monty Morgan with some enthusiasm.

"What is so calamitous about missing the first night of shore leave?" I said. "You have just two duty nights a week. The other five nights ought to be enough for you to service the entire distaff population of central California."

"You don't understand," said Fabian. "I have three tomatoes lined up for tonight to celebrate my return. They were going to pick up the check including a room at the Mark. Now, when I don't show . . . watch and see if some sixty-day Navy wonder doesn't wander in and usurp my entitlements. Some way to treat a defender of democracy."

"Get out of those party clothes," I said. "Put on your duty fatigues. We've got to clean up the ship; all the EM's will be ashore. Maybe some of them will run into your grateful paramours and all will not be lost—particularly the room deposit!"

"This is the sort of gratitude the war protestors thrive on. My reward for risking life and security to win the war in the South Pacific," said Fabian.

"Hey Fabian!" Lt. Baldwin shouted from the boat deck. "The cook went ashore with rest of the crew, and unless you know how to sauté the frozen quartermaster beef we are going to be dining on SPAM tonight."

"Executive talent is a terrible thing to waste," said Lt. Fabian Murphy.

As pilot Kevin Dockerdy had predicted, our reception at the San Francisco pier seemed to be following his script. Colonel Wilfred Margin came storming aboard with a chest full of ribbons that looked like a picnic serving of fruit salad. In the slow measured voice of a hanging judge, he began his inquiry:

"Do you realize that it took you longer to cross half the Pacific Ocean than it did Columbus to find the New World? What is your incredible explanation for this demonstration of incompetence and dereliction of duty?"

It was time to resort to Dockerdy's instructions. "Sir, we are fortunate to be here at all," I began. "We were put to sea with defective equipment known only to those who installed it. The lives of twenty men were at risk for almost five weeks because the Army neglected to inform us that our magnetic compass carried an additional twenty degrees of westerly deviation not shown on the correction card issued by the Manila vessel fitness authorities. Only the skill of our navigation officer, Lt. Monty Morgan, kept us from making landfall in Patagonia."

Snuffy was polishing the binnacle and now looked toward me and mouthed a "don't overdo it" message.

Colonel Margin, pride of the Artillery School until being transferred to the Transportation Corp., narrowed his eyes and said, "According to Capt. Drumond, your prior superior, this ship is noted for wild stories. When did you discover this error in the compass?

Fabian stepped forward. He had anticipated the question. "It was pilot Kevin Dockerdy," he said. "Dockerdy couldn't understand how we ended up in Seattle instead of San Francisco. He took the ship over the Navy's variation determination range and was shocked to discover twenty degrees of unrecorded westerly deviation. He was surprised we showed up at all."

The Colonel was not completely convinced. "I'll have a Navy instrument ordinance squad over here in the morning and I hope for the sake of your future, Captain, they can find this grievous error that kept you sailing in circles."

For the first time, Snuffy spoke up, "Sir, I don't think that would be the wisest thing to do. You know how eager the Navy is to spread the word that the Army is incapable of handling anything wetter than a damp wash rag. Within two hours, the entire pacific command will know that the Army can't install a dependable compass. We should keep this matter to ourselves."

The Colonel stared for a moment at the bulging-eyed little corporal, and then turned to me and said, "How do I know this compass story isn't another one of your cover-ups? This ship has become famous for its eyewash alibis. Where is the proof that you didn't just get lost in the woods?"

This was the part we had rehearsed. Taking Colonel Margin into the chartroom, I pointed out that the Alcatraz light lay at a bearing of two-hundred ten degrees from our position at the pier. Then I placed a bearing circle over the top of the compass bowl and set the sight vanes on the Alcatraz light. Colonel Margin squinted at the compass card and read two-hundred thirty degrees—twenty degrees westerly deviation!

The Colonel was convinced. "What do we do about it?" he cried. "If the Navy comes snooping around they will discover the problem and start making snide remarks about fish out of water."

Lt. Monty Morgan, ace navigator, straightened his slumped shoulders and announced in grave tones that there was a solution. "Since discovering the problem when we reached Seattle, I have been reviewing the principles of advanced physics which were so helpful to me when I was commodore of the Oyster Bay Yacht Club. I remember a similar occasion when . . ."

"I don't give a damn about the Oyster Bay Admirals," said the Colonel. "What about this compass? How soon can we have it pointing reasonably close to true North?"

This was Monty's moment. In a rubbery impersonation of General MacArthur accepting the Bronze Star, he said, "Within twenty four hours, sir."

With a look of no-confidence, the former National guardsman stepped close enough to fog the navigator's glasses. "You better make damn sure. If those Navy sand pounders find out about this snafu, I will be the guy on the receiving end of their smart-ass ridicule. The word is out that there is a star in the pipeline for me. If I don't make Brigadier because you guys can't distinguish the equator from a barber pole, you're going to wish you had been born without balls!" We watched him trip over a coiled line on the well deck as he headed for the gangway, snarling at the alert aide who had just kept him from repeating the dive from the FS344 in the Gulf of Mexico three years ago. Climbing into his staff car, we heard him order his driver, "Get me back to civilization!"

Snuffy watched the Colonel and his aide disappear behind the "Fin and Claw" restaurant, and then, doing a classic about-face, marched to the binnacle and pulled away the tape covering the fifty hearing aid batteries and unceremoniously dropped them overboard.

As the compass card slowly swung twenty degrees to the right, Snuffy snapped to attention in front of me. "Objective accomplished, sir. Compass deficiency corrected."

"It's about time," said navigating officer, Monty Morgan. "Now I can plot a true course and be assured that my dead-reckoning method will lay us at our objective with pin-point accuracy."

"Maybe you haven't noticed, Magellan, but we are fast to a pier right now", said Fabian. "With the exception of a garbage run, there is no indication that the Army is planning to send us anywhere other than the nearest mothball storage yard. If we do move out, try to take the pier with you. That way we will always know where we are when we run aground. Any shoal water we hit can be named Morgan's mistake. 'He added variation when he should have subtracted. He zigged when he should have zagged'."

Monty looked at Fabian as if he had stumbled over a toxic Florida toad. "You have been ashore less than two days and the word is out that you are organizing a USO chapter of 'Volunteer call girls'."

"Don't sneer at it," said Fabian Murphy. "It's the least we can do in the way of comfort and relaxation for the men who have spent the last three years risking their lives protecting those arm-chair admiral friends of yours back at the Newport Yacht Club. Have you priced a professional 'companion' lately? The government provides ten-cents a pack cigarettes for soldiers, a lot more dangerous than a clean cut 'volunteer' ready to do her part in the war effort."

"There could be a little danger if her husband finds out," said Lt. Baldwin, "Or she could have a weight-lifter boy friend who might frown on aid and comfort for the troops extended this far. Besides, there's a rumor that you are collecting an arrangement fee for the assignation."

"Merely for overhead," said Fabian. "This is a non-profit operation, purely for the GI's. Officers can make their own arrangements or come to me if they are shy. No free-bees for them, though. The ladies will be only officer-club-approved professionals, and guaranteed by career personnel to improve morale. Nothing in it for me. Just an opportunity to make a small contribution to the comfort of the deserving enlisted man. It's the least I can do. It may become a permanent branch of the USO – the VCC, 'Volunteer Comfort Companions'."

Life aboard ship in port was not what we had expected. Suddenly we learned there were regulations. It appeared there were more military inspectors than combat personnel. Snuffy said that if each inspector were required to kill one enemy, the war would have been over the first year.

The first citation we received was for out-of-uniform violations. Lt. Monty Morgan was wearing a hand-woven tartan-plaid kilt. His betrothed, Sylvia Raginfield, who had noted in her letter that the plaid was authentic and a reflection of the Morgan dynasty in the Highlands, had made it. Sylvia must have had John Wayne in mind when she was doing the tailoring. The waist was large enough to fit a barrelhead, and on Monty's scrawny frame only improvised suspenders could keep them above his knees. Seaman John Kaywood fashioned them from yellow canvas he found in the long boat, but without elastic they pulled the kilts up so high that Monty looked like a longhorn player in a Swiss opera. There was no reasoning with Colonel Margin. Monty said in the next war he would join Military Intelligence and wear clothes from Brooks Bros.

When Colonel Margin discovered Leondro Mattaxis and Aristotle Thalios were not wearing shoes, he was furious. "This ship is beginning to look like a banana boat," he roared. "Look at the Navy tanker moored aft of you—everybody in proper uniform, neat and proper, while you foul-ups sit here looking like rejects from the Grapes of Wrath."

"But sir," I protested. "They have a crew of eighty while we try to stay afloat with sixteen. Same size ship, but they do each other's laundry just to keep busy. We are lucky if our potatoes get peeled."

Leondro Mattaxis spoke up: "Colonel, Sir, Aristotle and I, in Greece, we stomp grapes in barefeet. Make very good wine. We bring you some soon. One day we stomp grape with shoes on. Foreman gets very mad. Fire us. Ever since we take off shoes if doing something important. Captain here, say everything we do is important, so we don't wear shoes. Wear shoes and ship might sink. Maybe Aristotle and I get fired again."

Aristotle Thalios decided to speak for himself. "Good to wear shoes when making love. If father come home too soon, shoes good to run fast on stones. Shoes good if dog tries to bite toes. No dogs on ship, so . . . ."

"Enough!" shouted Margin. "This bilge water is giving me a headache. I want this ship in compliance by 1200 hours tomorrow. Remember everything and person must look as if we are all on the same side. By the way Captain, I notice you are wearing mismatched socks."

"Hey," said Baldwin, "I got an identical pair! A perfect example of shoddy war-time manufacturing."

Margin wasn't finished. "Another thing I've noticed aboard this ship – no respect for authority or rank. I haven't seen a single salute. Does everyone have a sprained right arm?"

"It is the rough weather, sir," said Lieutenant Darrow. Darrow had completed two years of applied psychology and felt the question was in his court. "After three years of enduring gale force seas, these men have developed an opposing involuntary reflect that impedes any action of the right arm beyond shoulder height. The continuous grasping for life lines, bulkhead rails and other life-saving devices precludes the use of the right upper limb for normal routine motion."

Colonel Margin studied the dapper young officer briefly. "Lieutenant, please extend my sincerest sympathy to these valiant soldiers who now endure this unusual malady. I am confident that under your direction a cure will be effected soon. It is my suggestion that this be by noon tomorrow. Otherwise, further treatment will be administered by personnel at the guard house on Pier 14."

As Margin strode down the gangway, Fabian said to no one in particular, "Maybe we could cast off now and head back to Manila."

There was some good news. The charges of bigamy against Snuffy had been dropped. It seemed that the mayor of Carrabelle, Florida, whose daughter had married Snuffy in a ceremony performed by the Mayor, was not an ordained minister, so the marriage was invalid. "I have learned my lesson," said Snuffy. "Next time I will make sure the preacher is real. I will want to see his papers first."

"You may want to keep in mind your wife in Des Moines. Understand she still holds a legitimate certificate that says you are hers," said Fabian.

"I guess I'm just too sentimental," said Snuffy. "Getting married just seems the right thing to do when you are having an affair with a nice lady. It is the considerate thing to do. Right now I've got to practice saluting so Colonel Margin won't think I am thumbing my nose at him tomorrow."

The big inspection scheduled for noon the next day never took place. The crew, looking uncomfortable, was in clean uniforms for the first time. The Greeks were upset when Fabian made them remove the peacock feathers from their caps. "Very big in Greece," said Aristotle. "Means soldier is both a fighter and a lover. More lover than fighter because Greece is neutral country now."

"The inspectors are not up on all that legend jazz," said Fabian. "These guys might think it means you have been neutered. You wouldn't want that, would you?"

Both Aristotle and Leondro shouted, "No, No!" and ripped off the feathers.

It was well past noon with no sign of the inspection team when a messenger from TC headquarters came aboard and delivered orders instructing us to prepare to sail immediately. We were to proceed down the coast about a hundred miles to Rio Vista and await further orders. Fabian was ecstatic. "Our luck day," he exclaimed, "We get out of that chicken inspection and are being moved to Rio Vista. Never been there, but it sounds like one of those swinging resort spots. I'll check my book for phone numbers."

It felt good to be back at sea. No one to tell us what to wear or when to salute. Monty Morgan went back to his kilts. Our erstwhile lookout, Elwood Corbin, once again began reporting everything he saw, including a couple making out on the forward deck of a small sailboat as we moved past Fisherman's Wharf. Everything was going our way. We weren't lost, the weather was perfect, and we were heading to a berth where there wasn't even a military cantonment to ride our tail.

By running half-ahead, Engineer Cuthburt was able to stretch the trip to two days. Lookout Corbin reported a small spar buoy and wheelsman Kaywood swung the ship to port and up a short channel into a pond-like harbor. Something was wrong. There were no resorts or fishing piers in sight. Just rusting ships of every class, anchored side-by-side and abandoned. We were in a graveyard of ships.

It was hardly the reception we had anticipated after three years of battling the elements and risking permanent loss of our sense of direction. Lt. Darrow had said there would probably be a decommissioning ceremony where I would be required to wear a sword and scabbard. A band would play softly as the ensign was lowered and our ship entered its well-deserved retirement.

A small boat powered by a sputtering Evinrude outboard approached our port side. The lone occupant, a middle-age woman of ample proportions wearing a khaki home-guard uniform, asked permission to come aboard. There was some difficulty getting her up the short Jacobs ladder on to the boat deck. Aristotle and Leondro, our self-appointed Greek ambassadors, ever ready to assist anything wearing a skirt, rushed over to extend a helpful welcome.

"You very pretty lady," gushed Aristotle. "You have nice daughters at home, yes? Maybe they like to show Leondro and Aristotle how pretty Rio Vista. We bring flowers."

Our visitor ignored her ecumenical welcoming committee, turning to Private Elwood with a direct order, "Take me to your Captain, please."

Muriel Drexworthy was a volunteer member of the Army Ladies Auxiliary Harborcraft Unit. Her assignment, three days a week, was to meet incoming vessels and direct them to their designated berth. "Sort of like a parking lot attendant for ships," she explained. Our assigned spot was alongside an abandoned coal dock between a damaged World War I destroyer and an obsolete Coast Guard buoy tender.

"Sometimes I feel like a funeral director," said Muriel. "We know they will never sail again. Never be in open water until the Navy tows a couple to sea to serve as targets for a gunnery demonstration. Sad, but as my late husband always said, 'Death may be commonplace, but to each of us it's our own brief blaze of glory,' whatever that meant."

She was wrong about the FS344. None of us knew that the little ship that had kept most of us seasick for the past three years would rise again twenty-five years later as the ill-prepared PUEBLO, once more in a sea of confusion.

Fabian Murphy, always planning ahead in affairs of the heart, was eager to reconnoiter any unexplored territory. "Is RioVista a friendly place?" he said to Ms. Drexworthy. "Do they welcome service people just returned from hazardous duty?"

Muriel beamed. "Very friendly. Every Tuesday and Thursday afternoon there is a reception for servicemen at the First Presbyterian Church where we serve chicken salad sandwiches and rice pudding. Last year we were mentioned in Stars and Stripes as the place to be if your leave is canceled."

Fabian pressed on. "What about watering holes? I mean, like relaxing cocktail lounges where a guy can put aside thoughts of combat and dream of home."

"Oh, sure, there's the Pony Bar. Owned by Carl Drexel. Very nice place" said Muriel. "Carl keeps a three-gallon jar filled with pickled eggs on the bar. With every second beverage you get a free egg. Even coffee and sodas count. We have our ladies auxiliary meeting there every other Friday. Carl puts us in a private room so noise from the bar won't bother us. You know how loud men can be after a cold beer. Carl is trying to run a segregated establishment—you know men on one side, women on the other. Carl says everybody is more comfortable that way."

Fabian was becoming impatient. "To put it bluntly, Ms. Drexworthy, does RioVista have a list of professional call girls?"

Muriel stiffened. "I don't know what you are talking about," she said. "It's time to get this ship into the pier."

"Maybe they use volunteers," said Lt. Darrow.

Moving the ship into a space only slightly longer that the ship was a challenge. Muriel Drexworthy took Snuffy ashore to handling our docking lines. Aristole and Leondro prepared heaving lines for Snuffy to haul in the bow hauser. He neatly caught the monkey fist of the line and began rapidly hauling it in only to discover that, as once before, our Greek seaman had neglected to make the free end fast to the eye of the hauser. The ship drifted back out into the harbor. Muriel, watching from her Evinrude skiff murmured a prayer of thanks that the war was over.

Finally, after an afternoon of maneuvering, and secure at the pier, we were informed it would take a week to ten days to inventory the ship and process the reassignment of the personnel. The word "inventory" bothered me. I knew the captain was responsible for all government property and could be made liable for items damaged or missing. It was time to consult with Snuffy.

The little corporal blinked a couple of times and finally said, "Don't worry, we will use the FINO—First In Never Out—system. Always works." A supply sergeant at Fort Bragg perfected it. He discovered that he had an overage of six field jackets. Knowing that to the Army this was as serious as a shortage and that if he didn't come up with an acceptable explanation he might be demoted, he devised a solution—he took the jackets behind the barracks and burned them. Of course, we had a shortage, so we worked it in reverse—LINO. "Last In Never Out."

I was confused, "Wait a minute, corporal. We are going to be dealing with a professional bean counter. We are not going to snow him with some wacky formula dreamed up by a mixed up Fort Bragg sergeant. Besides, the plan sounds shady and I believe in honesty."

Stoic as usual, Snuffy blinked a few times and finally said, "You are right, skipper. Honesty is the best policy, particularly if you can afford it. You can speed things up and clear your conscience by telling that numbers-cruncher that you know there is plenty of government property missing and to bill you for it. Finance can take it out of your pay. It is one way of assuring yourself of a long military tenure."

"Tell me more about your plan," I said.

"Too complicated right now," said Snuffy. "Just let me have two crewmen and offer our services to the inventory detail. Explain we can be big help because we know where everything is stowed."

"What if they don't want you? What if they smell Greeks bearing gifts?" I said.

"They will jump at the offer," said Snuffy. "Remember we are all goldbricks at heart. Taking inventory is a boring job. Any help with the dirty work will be welcome. Of course we will be watched carefully. Those accountant types don't tolerate hanky-panky."

"Okay, you've got your men. Remember, the honor of this ship is at stake," I said.

"Whatever we do will be in accord with the tradition of this ship. Cross my heart," said Snuffy.

Warrant Officer Warren Willis headed a detail of three enlisted men assigned to inventory the FS344. He was grateful for the offer of assistance, but assured me that my crewmen would in no way be involved in the actual count but would be utilized in the more physical duties of producing and restoring the items being inventoried. He punctuated each sentence with a sniff which made me wonder whether he was allergic to salt air or was this some method of accounting. Like three sniffs meant thirty, or possibly a single sniff indicated doubt about the accuracy of client-provided figures. He then called my attention to his CPA license to assure me that his inventory would be accurate and beyond question. "The honor of my profession as a Certified Public Accountant must be upheld in all instances," he said in a sincere but quavering voice. Sniff or not, it was reassuring to know we were in capable hands.

Two days after the inventory began, Willis appeared at my cabin door and asked permission to enter. "I wish to congratulate you, Captain, on a most satisfactory inventory. You must have run a tight ship. There appears to be almost no shrinkage of the initial Government Issue of property." He was smiling and sniffing at the same time. "There was one irregularity that perhaps you could explain. The original issue of chipping hammers was thirty-six. We counted thirty-nine. Can you account for this overage?"

Fabian had joined us and jumped in. "Indeed we can, sir. I remember it like yesterday. It was in San Diego. We were moored side by side with the FS343 and both crews were doing their constant chipping and painting, slung over the side on scaffolds. Because the ships were so close, the crews were literally mingling and chipping hammers were being unintentionally interchanged. We ended up with three hammers belonging to the 343. Should have returned them."

Warrant Officer Warren Willis smiled. "I will try to remember that should I inventory the FS343, give them credit for three chipping hammers. One other minor discrepancy involved the bedsheets. You are short four bedsheets, but because you've picked up three chipping hammers, we will call it an off-set." He sniffed again and ducked his head. "Just a joke you know."

After Warrant Officer Willis left the ship I called in Snuffy. "You know we have lost over half our issued equipment. What happened with the bean counters?"

"Easy. We used LINO," said Snuffy. "Those inventory boys were good counters. They counted everything twice. I told the officer that after three years at sea stored items were scattered all over the ship. We offered to take them to all the right areas if necessary, move the stuff to a central location for their convenience. They thanked us for our consideration. We kept bringing the same items back. We counted the chipping hammers in the bowpoint locker. Then, while the detail was working its way, my boys moved the hammers to storage lockers in the stern. Got a little mixed up and moved three too many. Warrant Officer Willis said if I ever needed a reference, use his name."

Only three days in port and we had worn out our welcome. Lt. Ronald Cuthburt, erudite chief engineer, had been returned to the ship by the Military Police after challenging the patrons of a local bar to a dual to be fought with sabers after someone suggested that General Braxton Bragg of the Confederacy lacked the military ability of Ulysses S. Grant at Chickamauga.

Grabbing a pool cue and leaping to the top of the billiard table, Cuthburt announced that not only was he going to defend the honor of the South, he planned to rid the world of all those who had not read the completed works of Shakespeare, unabridged, of course.

The two MP's who brought our inebriated officer of culture and good taste back to the ship warned us that one more incident like this and we would be sailing without a chief engineer. An idle threat because we knew the FS344 would never sail again.

Muriel Drexworthy came aboard to report in a most diplomatic way that Lt. Fabian Murphy had not behaved like an officer and a gentleman in the Pony Bar last night. According to the report Muriel had received, after his second daiquiri, he made inappropriate suggestions to the waitress, proposing that after closing she accompany him back to the ship to inspect the officers' quarters and see for herself how unsuitable living conditions were for the men who guarded the United States under the most hazardous circumstances. She might be moved enough to write her congressman.

Lt. Darrow spoke up in Fabian's defense "Mrs. Drexworthy, all sailors take harmless liberties their first night ashore. Fabian probably used that line on every female he met that evening, and hoped no one would accept. He wouldn't know what to do if they did. No harm in making an innocent pass at a good-looking waitress."

"There is plenty of harm when the good-looking waitress happens to be the wife of the owner of the Pony Bar – Carl Drexel!" said Muriel.

It was time to bring the discussion to a close. "I will speak to Lt. Murphy today," I promised. "Be assured there will be no further incidents of this nature. Please extend our deep apologies to Carl Drexel and his wife."

Muriel had other items on her list. "Last night at the USO Canteen there was this little red-headed soldier with bulging blue eyes."

"Sounds like Snuffy," said Darrow.

"Seemed a little weird," said Muriel. "He proposed marriage to every girl in the place. Even Marjorie Happlestead, the chaperone, our city librarian. When they rejected his offer, he thanked them."

I tried to explain. "Snuffy is a soldier with a conscience. He feels that should he score there will be some legitimacy to the affair because he had proposed marriage in advance – sort of moral responsibility in reverse."

"Incredulous," said Mrs. Drexworthy. "You have a strikingly odd crew, Captain. Those two wild Greeks of yours have every father in town buying chastity belts for their daughters. Was it a problem finding these psycho candidates in one place?"

"You are misjudging us." I said. "You must recognize that we have been at sea for almost three years. For the first time we don't have to walk on bulkheads or sleep with a lifeline in place to keep from falling on the deck. I know we are all acting strange – Fabian, Darrow, Baldwin, Morgan, myself."

Muriel interrupted, "How can you include Monty, I mean Lt. Morgan, in generalization of this peculiarly odd group? Lt. Morgan is a considerate and understanding gentleman, an intellectual with an understanding of the true meaning of life. Without him you and your crew would probably still be floundering around trying to find the American Continent."

"Thank you Mrs. Drexworthy, I will apologize to our navigator," I said. "He certainly is different from the rest of us."

Lt. Darrow and I watched Muriel pick her way across the well deck trying to avoid the clutter of cleats, shackles, swivels and other debris left by a work detail when Monty Morgan interrupted their routine with a short lecture on the Cambrian Period, a time in the Paleozoic Era when a profusion of marine animals was first noted. With the smug look of an Isaac Newton after formulating the laws of gravity and motion, Monty straightened his scrawny frame and brought his lecture to a conclusion with, "Today, you can see for yourself the descendants of the world's first geological period – the trilobites and brachiopods. Inspect the hull of our ship just below the water line, and there they are: BARNACLES!

Muriel Drexworthy applauded. The work crew looked disappointed. They had hoped for a longer break.

Monty turned toward Muriel and murmured a humble, "Thank you."

"So wonderful," gushed Muriel," to enlighten our boys in service with your knowledge of the past's culture and our place in the universe. You must agree to appear at our next Ladies Volunteer Auxiliary Meeting. Will you promise?"

Monty modestly lowered his head and softly said," I could bring my Lepidoptera collection, butterflies, you know."

"My God," said Darrow, "they're in love!"

Lt. Baldwin had joined us. "I heard her say that Monty reminded her of her late husband."

"She must have been married to a scarecrow," said Fabian.

Ronald Cuthburt, Chief Engineer, sober for the moment and looking as somber as a born-again judge, spoke up: "This could be serious, gentlemen. If the scion of the Morgan dynasty forsakes his betrothed, the heir to the Raginfield fortune, there could be a Wall Street collapse. Investment bankers would shudder, and those handling the Morgan trust might want to resign."

"What has that got to do with us?" I said. "Are we suppose to be the Beatrice Fairfax of the Pacific Theatre? Nobody got excited when Snuffy almost went to jail over his out-of-control marital peccadillo's."

Our Harvard-educated engineering officer became more pragmatic about the matter. "Snuffy did not control half the capital on the Northeast coast. His marriages were the results of trying to legitimize lust. Monty's future merging of big-time fortunes was planned and approved around a board table in the financial section of lower Manhattan. Bust those plans and you and this crew could fine themselves in deep trouble."

Lt. Darrow found Cuthburt's scenario incredulous. "What are you talking about! We have taken care of Monty ever since he came aboard. He should have been keelhauled the third time he ran us aground. Fabian even saved him from drowning!"

It was time for me to make a decision. "Call in Snuffy," I ordered.

After fourteen years in service during which time he had spent more time in the guardhouse than on the parade ground, Pvt. Snuffy had been promoted to corporal. We suspected that in someway Snuffy Elliot had maneuvered his own promotion. His own worst enemy, yet invaluable to those who commanded him. He provided sage advice to officers who had never learned how to unravel military red tape or understand formal orders from headquarters. He recognized weaknesses in others and used them to shift an opinion in his direction. In an argument, you were doomed. The obvious always seemed to be on his side. The officer-enlisted relationship had to be handled gingerly. It was rank's privilege to make the right decision and for the enlisted consul to agree. Snuffy was master at seeing that the discussion was going in his direction so he could agree and compliment the officer on his wise decision. All of us knew it was Snuffy's ball game, but why tamper with tradition? We took the credit.

Snuffy listened to the Monty Morgan story and agreed with Lt. Cuthburt that we were in an uncomfortable position if Monty rejected the anointed Sylvia Raginfield and made off with full-figured Muriel Drexworthy. "The Morgan clan is pretty touchy about marriage outside the compound and the dissolution of the family fortune. Their motto carved in oak is 'Live it up, but don't touch the principal'."

"Where do we come in?" asked Baldwin.

"As scapegoats," said Snuffy. "The family with all its wealth and contributions to the right political parties, will want to cover its tracks by using its influence at the Pentagon and enlisting the DOD to place the blame on the lack of officer discipline aboard the FS344. You officers will be accused of encouraging fraternization with undesirable company and not properly supervising the off-duty activities of those under the captain's command. Nothing really serious but enough to get each of you a letter of criticism in your 201 file precluding any promotions. Might even jeopardize your military pension."

"Enough, already," said Lt. Darrow. "How do we get this thing off our backs and get on to a simpler life like keeping Fabian from being arrested for attempted rape?"

"You are confused," said Fabian. "If I can't be charged with standard rape, I want no part of it."

Snuffy came back to the primary problem: "The only way we can put out Monty's flame is to discredit Muriel Drexworthy."

"You mean like a drunk driving charge, or a cocaine bust, or maybe an overdue pledge of citizen loyalty?" said Baldwin.

"No, no," said Snuffy. "Charges like that would only produce sympathy with Lt. Morgan. You have got to hit where it hurts – her background in history. Right now she claims she can trace her lineage back to John C. Fremont, founder of the California Republic. I think that is what Monty fell in love with."

"What is the next step?" I said.

Snuffy looked around the group and pointed at Fabian. "Lt. Murphy must know some unscrupulous investigator in Boston who would do a background check for one of the Lieutenant's confidential investment tips. Nobody is without warts somewhere."

"I know just the guy," said Fabian, "and he owes me one. Tell him what you want him to find and he will have it documented within twenty-four hours. Did one on the Pope last year. Chip in for the telephone call now and I'll have his report by Wednesday. Great slogan: 'If you need a reputation, see us'."

Questioning Fabian about his unofficer—like behavior at the Pony Bar was like asking a kleptomaniac why he preferred shopping at self-service department stores. "How did I know she was the owner's wife?" he said. "She should have worn a name tag - - 'property of the house', or 'off-limits except to big-tippers.' Besides, she was coming on to me. Brought me a pickled egg and didn't put it on the check. Wouldn't that imply that she wanted to be more than another cute waitress in your life?"

"Everyone at the Pony Bar gets a free pickled egg with the second drink. It's a marketing gimmick," I said. "If it was an invitation to sex, those girls would be the busiest waitresses in California. Carl Drexel hands out about one-hundred twenty eggs a night. Even you couldn't keep up with that."

Fabian was impressed. "Great sales incentive! Well, no harm done. I will get over to Carl's and apologize for misunderstanding his wife's hospitality. Give me a chance to discuss with him the new services I am underwriting: '84 Ways the Small Business Man Can Double His Net Without Paying Taxes'. I am expecting an early discharge soon, so thought I better start laying the groundwork for an international service that will benefit the small investor and assure a future of comfort and security for his heirs. Not much in it for me, except the satisfaction of knowing that in a small way I have helped make this a better world."

"Beautiful," I said. "I guess if you can't have Carl Drexel's wife, you'll settle for his bank balance, but count me out. I am planning on the proletarian life-style with government savings bonds in the mattress."

Fabian displayed the compassionate side of his nature. "This country needs people like you, Skipper. People willing to sacrifice the comforts of the world to provide opportunities for the rest of us. Think of me as an expediter, leading the uniformed to a future of prosperity and well-being—sort of a Moses with only the welfare of his people in mind."

"Moses, expedite that background report on Muriel Drexworthy so we can lead Monty Murphy not unto temptation."

As promised, Fabian delivered Muriel Drexworthy's background check Wednesday morning to my quarters. It was a comprehensive review of exemplary behavior, detailing the many occasions of volunteerism when Muriel sought to improve the lot of both the individual and the community. Her contribution to the war effort was outstanding. She organized the local USO chapter, sold War Bonds at the service clubs, and set up blood-collecting stations at every church in the county. She could trace her ancestry back to John C. Fremont, liberator of California from Mexico.

"This review would make Florence Nightingale feel inadequate," said Lt. Baldwin. "Monty will want to make her head of the House of Morgan five minutes after he reads it."

"You haven't read the last paragraph," said Fabian.

Baldwin began reading the final few lines aloud: "Ms. Drexworthy's great-great grandfather on her Mother's side was Ephran Duvenack, a rebel leader in the 1794 Whiskey Rebellion in Pennsylvania. He was convicted of treason but later pardoned."

"That's it!" said Darrow. "Monty's squeeze has a traitor on the family tree, a rebel trying to bring down the government the Morgan's fought to establish."

"How do we get the report to Monty without him recognizing our hand in digging up the dirt?" said Cuthburt.

"No problem," said Fabian. "I have been trying to interest Muriel in considering a sensational new annuity plan for young widows and single women. I will tell Monty that the underwriting company requires a background check and that Muriel Drexworthy's report was so glowing I made a copy for him because of his interest in the lady."

That afternoon Monty accepted the report from Fabian and thanked him for his interest. "No problem," said Fabian. "Makes you proud to know a person so squeaky clean."

It was just after we had finished a connoisseur's shipboard dinner at the captain's table, consisting of canned spaghetti and frozen meatballs, when Monty asked to meet with me privately in my quarters.

"Don't expect absolution for the six times you got us lost," said Fabian. "You got Corporal Melos Crawford singing those sad songs of his until we thought perdition had finally found us."

Monty did not respond. Looking more like a chipmunk than usual, he headed for my cabin where I found him slumped on the only chair in the room. I leaned on the upper bunk and hoped the meeting would be short. The meatballs were beyond the safe-serving date because quartermaster had ordered our cook to serve all the remaining food on board before we were mustered out. I needed the Pepto Bismo but Snuffy had mixed it with the vanilla extract for a clandestine celebration when we made landfall at Seattle.

"Can we hurry this up?" I said. "I really need to rest my back. Been climbing more ladders since we have been at dock than when we were at sea. Snuffy says the motion of the sea makes it easier to go up and down a ladder. Those outdated meatballs aren't helping."

Monty Morgan made no move to give up the chair. Just continued to peer over the top of his wire-rims with the expression of a defrocked member of Sons of the American Revolution. He offered a cigarette, which I declined. "Can we hurry this up?" I pleaded, "my back is killing me."

"Get these for ten cents a pack from quartermaster. Use them for tips in restaurants. Save money. Waitresses go wild for them because they can't buy them on the civilian market. You would be shocked to know what they offer for a carton. Soap is another item better than silver. Fabian gets a full night on the town with a six-pack of bath soap."

"Look, Monty," I said, "as long as I can't have the chair, let's get to the point. Are you in trouble? Got somebody in a family way?"

"It's Muriel Drexworthy," said Monty.

"You've got Muriel pregnant! Incredible!"

"No, No," he said. "It's a matter of honor. I've implied to Muriel that I am considering a proposal of marriage. She is a wonderful lady, you know. She can trace her ancestor's back to the founders of California. One fought against the Spaniards. Ideal lineage."

"So what is the problem?" as if I didn't know.

"Today I received this exemplary background report and discovered that unbeknown to her, there was a blight on the family tree, a blackguard who rebelled against our early government. A traitorous individual ready to bring down the government our forefathers had fought so valiantly to establish."

"So what has that got to do with Muriel? Is she planning to start a protest of her own against the high taxes on booze as her early relative did when he discovered the new government taking a share of the profits he made from his home brew?"

"You don't understand," said Monty. "The Morgans enjoy a neat whiskey on occasion as everyone else, but they will never accept into the family a person without an impeccable ancestorial history. Muriel knew nothing about it until I showed her the report. She was as shocked as I was. What do I do now?"

"You may want to discuss the matter with Lt. Murphy, our morale officer. He has had lots of experience with matters of the heart and could probably arrive at a rational solution to your problem."

"I wouldn't discuss an ingrown toenail problem with Fabian Murphy!" he cried. "His idea of the difference between right and wrong is which is the most profitable – for him. More fitting if we called him our 'demoralizing officer'."

I decided to cut the meeting short. My back was killing me and I needed that chair. "Look, Monty, face up to this problem. Tell Muriel a union of the two of you is impossible. Might even cause a collapse of the New England financial world. Point out that like Caesar's wife, a bride of a Morgan must be without reproach – for at least two-hundred years. You might even offer to make her your mistress, but nothing on paper. You are a pretty smooth operator. You can do a sort of Madam Butterfly ending, emphasizing your sacrifice in upholding the honor of the Morgan dynasty. Now, get over to Muriel's place and let me have the chair."

Watching the FS344 being decommissioned was like witnessing a flock of crows cannibalize roadkill on the turnpike. The first to go was the armament – the two-inch gun on the foredeck and the two fifty-caliber machine guns on the flying bridge. The detail was puzzled by the twelve-degree bend in the barrel of the starboard machine gun. The sergeant in charge was impressed. "You guys must have been in few hot skirmishes to melt down a barrel like this," he said.

"It was touchy," admitted Monty. "When you are in the thick of things you forget some of the rules – like firing in bursts to keep the piece cool."

"Tell him about the attacking seagull you finally brought down," said Fabian. "The one that was after our Oreo cookies."

Next to go were the two gigantic life rafts, mounted at a forty-five-degree angle just forward of the bridge obscuring our vision in tight quarters. Wonderful excuse for wiping out misplaced piling and small boats. The removal of the navigation equipment distressed Monty who wanted to keep the sextant. Monty explained to the sergeant that the Long Island Yacht Club planned to mount the instrument in the Club's foyer with a modest plague mentioning the service-above-self action taken by Lt. Monty Morgan in bringing the FS344 safely across the ocean. The sergeant was unyielding. His orders said all navigation equipment to be removed and that included sextants. To lessen the pain of disappointment, Fabian offered Monty an old Boy Scout knife with a compass in the handle. "A little rusty but you could bronze plate it and tell those armchair admirals that a skilled navigator like a Morgan can locate his position by holding a wet finger in the wind."

Monty ignored Fabian's humor and asked permission to leave the ship, explaining that he had an important appointment ashore that afternoon. All of us knew he was on his way to see Muriel. "Maybe he will buy her off with a half interest in the Boston Red Sox," said Lt. Darrow.

When Monty burst into my room that night, I grabbed the lone chair. My back was still aching and I was determined to be comfortable if Monty decided to go into overtime while unburdening his soul.

"She understood!" he began. "She is a wonderful woman. There were no tears, nothing said to make me feel reprehensible. We agreed that we could have a delightful life together, but that blight in her past, almost two-hundred years ago, would always be with us. It just wouldn't be fair to the children, if there were any. Proud as they would be of the Morgan name, the shadow of treason and the Whiskey Rebellion of 1784 would always be in their closet. Public office would be out of the question."

Monty's expression of abject remorse brought back memories of our neighborhood morticians, Siebolt & Marintette, whose ingrained look of sadness never left them. When Siebolt won the Catholic Church's five-thousand dollar lottery, he accepted his prize with the depressed look of Charles I heading for the block. Monty's wire rims slid down his nose and for a moment I thought he might begin to cry; then he brightened.

"I think I may write a book about my adventures and the part I played in protecting the government my forefathers fought so valiantly to established. The Chamber at Martha's Vineyard will probably publish it and sell the book to tourists coming to look at the Morgan estate."

"Getting back to Muriel Drexworthy," I said, "did you give her a parting gift—roses, chocolates, or maybe a bottle of Chanel Number Five?"

"I gave her my butterfly collection," said Monty.

When Fabian heard the news he took full credit for preserving the Morgan dynasty. "It was my background check that kept the east coast monetary system from going down the tubes, and saved our butts. Those banking trust officers might have charged us with influencing Monty, and taken their beef to the Department of Defense. With their suction we would probably be reduced in rank and lose our separation pay."

"I guess we owe a lot to you," I said with some sarcasm. "That report, how was the insurance company able to dig back to the 1700s and come up with all that Whiskey Rebellion stuff?"

Morale officer Fabian Murphy shifted his position on my bunk, and looking around to be certain there were no witnesses. "They didn't. I added that."

I was shocked. "That is terrible," I said. "That is defamation of character. You could be sued for that!"

"Don't sweat it," said Fabian. "Everybody knows there was this joker who raised hell because the Feds wanted a slice of his home brew profits. Besides, Muriel's background turned out to be so much without sin that Monty would want to build a platform for her. Even Muriel was surprised to learn that two-hundred fifty years ago this farmer joined her family tree. Who is going to prove he didn't? She was so impressed with the thoroughness of the background check that she is going to invest in the Widows' Annuity program I prepared for her. Says that any insurance company that exacting must be very reliable."

Carl Drexel, proprietor of the Pony Bar, was not as understanding. He sent word that Fabian could patronize his establishment, but would no longer be provided with the complimentary pickled eggs.

It was the morning of October 12, 1946, while the crew was scrubbing down the decks for the last time when orders were delivered transferring all of us to Transportation Corps headquarters at Fort Eustis, Virginia. There was no decommissioning ceremony, just a neat packet for each person with orders and railway tickets and four days of food vouchers. We were required to be packed and at the station in three hours. No sentimental farewells. When Lt. Cuthburt reached the end of the gangway, he turned toward the tired-looking FS344 and said, "Thanks for the most miserable three years of my life," and he tossed one of his verboten bottles of bourbon into the harbor.

"The closest I ever want to be near water again," said Lt. Darrow, "is the Tunnel of Love at Laguna Park in Cleveland. The last thing I will consider will be a cruise vacation. Think of the money I'll save."

Monty Morgan was more philosophical. "This ship and I are symbols of seaworthiness and outstanding navigation. We will probably be mentioned in textbooks as examples of dedication to the preservation of our nation, always on the ready, regardless of hardship or personal safety."

"Except when you were seasick," said Fabian. "We were safer when you were in your bunk than when you were in the chart room trying to decide which went up or down — longitude or latitude. Didn't matter though, because you could always prove we were on water."

Snuffy, peering through the late afternoon haze at the ship that had been his home for the past three years, showed no remorse over the parting. "Makes no difference," he said. "Whether I am at sea or on the beach, it's a sure bet I'll be in trouble." Snuffy's appearance never seemed to change; a five-foot-six figure, a bleached white face with hundreds of maroon freckles competing for space with a pair of popping pale blue eyes, and always a quizzical expression implying a solution for every illogical problem. "The best defense is confusion," he would say. "Always quote from the Army manual – 'page 1723 – bar 3-C,' a section no one has ever found. Your examiner will never admit he doesn't know what you are talking about. It's your turn on the offensive. Remember, it is better to know some of the questions than all the answers."

It was time to express gratitude for the little corporal's counsel when there seemed to be no acceptable answers.

"Don't thank me," said Snuffy. "It was an opportunity to feel worthwhile, applying common logic to ridiculous military problems. If I had been able to do it for myself for the past fifteen years I might have been able to make buck

Sargent. I know we will probably never see each other again, but if the Army starts squeezing you, try to get in touch. I may have some guard house logic that will get them off your back."

I watched him walk down the pier, an unimposing small figure who advised and guided those who out-ranked him with the logic that he was unable to apply to himself. An intellectual born loser, never able to get beyond the rank of corporal.

An Army bus took us to the station where we boarded a train scheduled to reach Richmond, Virginia, four days later. Two MP's informed me that as ranking officer I would be responsible for the behavior of all military personnel aboard. It was like FS344 revisited. The first night out we were busy pulling two Greeks, Aristotle and Leondro, out of other passengers' berths. "Only being friendly," explained Aristotle. "Young ladies very scared on train alone. We protect them. Greeks like to help people."

"You 'help' any more people and the MP's will lock you in the baggage car for the rest of the trip," I warned. "Lt. Cuthburt is already there for trying to serve mint juleps to a group of bank examiners."

Fabian kept busy selling orange groves in Mexico to a group of newly graduated accountants. "They are the best prospects," he said. "If the numbers add up, they are interested."

"Did you mention the Mediterranean fruit fly?" I said.

"That's one-in-a-hundred year risk," he said. I hoped that someone told the fruit fly. Lt. Darrow and Snuffy ran a forbidden poker game under a blanket in the small lounge adjoining the men's room.

The train arrived in Richmond at six in the morning and the men were anticipating a carefree day in town. Fabian had pulled out six ripe telephone numbers from his "friendship" book and offered to share them – for a small fee, of course. As we stepped off the train we were met by the driver of a military bus ready to transport us to Fort Eustis. The military police on the train had recommended to headquarters that we not be given a day of liberty in Richmond, but be assigned to duty as soon as convenient. Fabian threatened to call his friends at the Pentagon.

Kevin Woodbridge, warrant officer, junior grade, was at the Richmond station with orders to escort the personnel of the FS344 to Transportation Headquarters at Fort Eustis for evaluation and further assignment. It was apparent from his manner when he received us that he was in some awe in the presence of sixteen battle-hardened veterans just returned from the Pacific Wars.

Snuffy had advised us not to polish the brass on our uniforms. "Leave the buttons sea-air green," he said. "Take the stiffeners out of your headgear. The hanger-based air-jockeys have been getting away with this for years, even though regs say the only exception to wearing headgear as issued is when it is necessary to use earphones. Makes a great impression. Looks like you have just come out of a dogfight with the Red Baron at thirty-thousand feet. Even MacArthur likes the look. Been told that his orderly stomps on the Commander's hat every morning to make it look properly battle-abused before the camera crews show up."

The only camera we saw when we disembarked from the Seaboard Southern Train was a pocket Kodak in the hands of warrant officer Kevin Woodbridge who insisted on having his own picture taken standing next to the legendary navigator, Monty Morgan. This display of profound respect was a heady experience for those of us who had begun to think that the threat of disciplinary action was like the required viewing of the VD warning films--pleasure now, perdition later.

"I will never have the chance to see combat action," said W.O. Woodbridge. "I stayed in school too long. The war was over on the day I received my appointment. You guys were lucky. Got in early and had the opportunity to get into the thick of it, build a war record."

Fabian decided it was time to get some mileage out of all this deserved recognition of valor. "Don't envy us," he said. "It wasn't wine and roses. The real heroes are those who are still out there. We are the lucky ones, regardless of what we went though. Look at Private Elliot. He will probably carry that limp for the rest of his life."

Actually, Snuffy had been struck on the ankle with a pool cue when the train had been held over in St. Louis for two hours and he had found a bar within walking distance.

Kevin understood our reluctance to discuss war experiences." While you men were risking your lives to preserve a way of life for the rest of us, I was draft-deferred to complete a university research project– 'Sex Life of Flowers at High Altitudes'."

Lt. Darrow was impressed." Fabian could have helped you on that. He once knew a girl named Iris. Her father brought his research project to a fast halt."

"All of you must have some great stories to tell," said Kevin. "I suppose a few of you have the Purple Heart. I notice that none of you are wearing your decorations today".

"Too painful," said Lt. Baldwin. "Each ribbon is a reminder that we are here today because of a friend's sacrifice. We have vowed not to glorify ourselves while others stood fast and took the blows meant for us."

It was time to bring this self–effacing discussion to a close. Chief engineer, Ronald Cuthburt had wandered off to find an open bar in the terminal. Apparently he was successful for now he was showing signs of arrogance and challenging anyone who wished to debate the tactics of Confederate General James Longstreet at the battle of Chickamauga in 1863. Kevin Woodbridge was concerned about this unusual behavior until Fabian whispered, "Shell shock and a touch of malaria. Poor devil, will probably be confined to a veteran's hospital."

"I understand," said Kevin. "Another price to be paid for victory. What is he doing now?"

Lt. Cuthburt was standing on one of the waiting room benches, his distinguished white hair flipping from side to side as he cried, "Braxton Bragg is back. The South will rise again!"

It was time to assert my rank. "Warrant Officer Woodbridge, get this detail on the bus before we end up losing our medals of honor."

At Fort Eustis we were greeted by a hard-bitten, no-nonsense young captain who informed us that although the war was over we were still in the Army and subject to its regulations. Fabian was not impressed. "Wait until I'm back in personnel," he whispered." "He will be a latrine inspection officer on Okinawa before he can get his shirts back from laundry."

At Regimental headquarters we were informed that the Transportation Corps was forming a water division and that we would be responsible for the publication of training material to prepare recruits for sea duty. My staff would include Monty Morgan, Fabian Murphy, and Lts. Darrow and Baldwin. In view of our extensive sea duty we were assigned to write and publish manuals on ship handling, navigation, rules of the road, maneuvering information, cargo stowage, rescue procedures, and "station keeping," whatever that meant.

Lt. Baldwin was skeptical. "How can we write training manuals on subjects we are not certain how to spell? We could get a copy of our ship's log and recommend doing the opposite, or, if that doesn't work, use prayer."

Fabian, as usual was more upbeat. "Hey, these sand pounders asking for this stuff don't know anymore about marine matters than we do. If they did they wouldn't need us. We can do some wheel spinning and keep the project going until they run out of funds or we are separated from the service." Fabian leaned back and waited for applause.

"Won't work," I said. "Lt. Col. Harvey Thompson, our project supervisor, wants completed outlines on every subject within 60 days. He is a former Madison Avenue ad agency guy and expects deadlines to be met. He also wants plans for 22 extension courses to be used for at-home training of reservists. Big assignment for a bunch of guys who just learned that a sailor never spits into the wind. Wish Snuffy was here to solve this one for us."

Lt. Monty Morgan suddenly came to life and peering over his wire-rims said, "I have the answer to your unpleasant problem."

"What's your solution, Monty? Use the Morgan fortune to buy off Colonel Thompson and get him to forget the whole thing?" said Lt. Darrow.

Ignoring the frivolous nature of Darrow's remark, Monty continued, "I will get in touch with Harvey Rackham, commandant of the Long Island Yacht Club, and ask him to send me his copy of Knights Modern Seamanship. Eight hundred and forty-six pages of everything from anchors to yardarms. We can take it chapter by chapter and have twenty-two outlines in a couple of weeks."

"Sounds like plagiarism to me," said Baldwin. "Austin M. Knight might recognize his stuff and tip off the War Department."

Fabian was more upbeat. "Plagiarism is when you copy something that isn't true. Knight's stuff is authentic because he probably copied it from the memoirs of Admiral Farragut who could have lifted all he knew from John Paul Jones. Let us be sure we are not copying somebody's mistakes. That would be plagiarism of the worst kind."

Commandant Rackham sent Monty the Long Island Yacht Clubs only copy of Knight's Modern Seamanship, Tenth Edition, along with a slim volume of "Rules of the Road for the Junior Naval Cadet." Receiving the later book pleased Monty. He had been a member of the Junior Cadet Corps. when he was fourteen and this textbook prepared him for his position as navigator on the FS344.

Within three weeks we presented to LTC Thompson outlines for twenty-two seamanship manuals. He squinted at them briefly and said, "From what source did you copy these?"

I protested with some indignation. The injustice of his question was an affront to our self-respect. Thompson grinned at us for a moment and seemed to enjoy our discomfort.

"Look, I was a Big Ten ad agency account executive on Madison Avenue for fourteen years. I learned early that you give the client what he wants to hear whether it is your idea of original thinking or his Mother-in-law's in-put from the bridge table. Bottom line: he is picking up the tab and your job is to make sure you are both on the same track."

"What about our outlines. Are they scuttled?" asked Baldwin.

"Of course not" said Thompson. "I'm sending them up the line and they will be inspected by every would-be marine experts from here to Corps. Headquarters. You won't recognize them when they get back, but it doesn't matter. You write the final manuals as you initially planned them. If they pass muster everybody but you will do a lot of back-scratching and take full credit for producing a state-of-the-art-training aid. If they get a thumbs down you will be recognized as the authors of unintelligible, if not dangerous, training material. It will be recorded in your 201 file, and you can be certain that your present rank is your permanent one."

"Sounds like a no-win scenario," said Fabian.

"Exactly", said Thompson, "but isn't that normal when we are all bucking for approval and promotion? However, a street-wise guy like you, Lieutenant, ought to be able to figure out a way around the system that will have you looking like a hero."

"I'll do my best," said Fabian.

"Sure you will," said Darrow, "while the rest of us dangle from the yardarm."

There was some good news. I received a promotion to Major with a commendation for not losing a single life to enemy action.

"That's because we never saw the enemy," grumbled Fabian. "Better not tell them that Monty almost wiped us all out with that runaway machine gun. He would have too if the barrel hadn't melted and jammed the piece."

"Don't be bitter," said Ronald Cuthburt. "You made more money than a major just by cheating the rest of us in your crooked poker games."

Headquarters provided us with a very adequate office, equipped with three IBM typewriters and two attractive civilian stenographers. "This assignment is going to be more interesting than I anticipated," said Fabian.

The only equipment we seemed to be missing was paper clips. After receiving no response from several requests, I decided to assign the problem to Lt. Fabian Murphy. Obtaining a supply of paper clips would keep him busy and away from the stenographers. His first move, of course, was to ask the stenographers to bring from their homes any extra clips they might have around the house. He even offered to help them search their bedrooms. A note from one of their fathers thwarted this well-meaning endeavor.

Next, Fabian decided to apply his considerable maneuvering ability in Army administration to obtain the clips we needed so badly. He submitted formal requests to Service of Supply, Battalion Headquarters, Regimental Support Services, and even the Quartermaster Corps. at the Pentagon. His messages were not only urgent, but occasionally threatening. Fabian Murphy was not a person to ignore.

After five weeks of no response, it finally happened. We received a modest-sized box containing five cases of paper clips. We were elated and congratulated Fabian on the successful completion of his assignment. A week later a delivery of twenty-four cases of paper clips arrived at our office.

"Must have been a goof-up at the procurement office," said Fabian. The following week a box marked, "one gross-paper clips" arrived at the office before we opened. We stored it next to Fabian's desk. Before the end of the month we had received 600 gross packages of paper clips. We were running out of storage space. It had become like the machine that made the ocean salty—we couldn't shut it off.

Fabian suggested we give the paper clips to the civilian employees to take home for their personal use, but it was quickly pointed out that government property can not be given away. Paper clips were arriving daily. On the day we were ordered to Fort Belvoir for separation, an army four-by-four truck was pulling up to our entrance. "My God! Let's get out of here fast," said Baldwin. "It's paper clips!"

We began work on the home extension courses for the inactive reservists. This was more relaxing because Lt. Col. Thompson told us they would be accepted as written. No sharp shooting from above.

Then without warning we were ordered to report to Fort Belvoir for separation from active duty, and separation from each other. Snuffy was ordered to Fort Riley in Kansas where he would serve three more years to make up for having walked away from the Army in 1938. Once again he offered to help me if I ever needed his sage advice. "Just get in touch," he said. "Might be in the guardhouse."

Ron Cuthburt, alcohol dependent, marine engineer, was offered a position on an Army Harborcraft salvage tug at New Orleans. We learned a year later that he was in an Army rehab center after having opened the sea cocks while the tug was at dockside in Mobile, Alabama.

Both Darrow and Baldwin returned to college on the GI Bill. Darrow to Stanford and Baldwin to Baltimore University to prepare further to take over his father's insurance business.

Our two Greek crewmembers, Leondro Mattaxis and Aristotle Thalios, were given the choice of becoming U.S.

citizens or transportation back to Greece. After a ninety-second consultation, their decision was to remain and become citizens. "Maybe we become gigolos," said Leondro. "Very big in Greece and Aristotle good dancer. Leondro, I good talker. Say nice things, make ladies very happy." As they walked away I noticed both were wearing flowers in their garrison caps.

Elwood Corbin, full-time lookout, re-enlisted. On the personnel information form under occupation or profession, Elwood listed his skill as "Lookout-first class."

The Morgan limousine was being sent down to Virginia to pick up Monty and return him to the family compound on Martha's Vineyard. He was making a clean break from the Army. "I've performed my duty with honor," he said. "I am really Navy and the Island Sailing Club has been holding open the office of commandant for me. No compensation, of course, but great privilege and recognition."

"Well, at least they are paying you what you are worth," said Fabian. "Hey, Monty, will you be inviting us to the wedding?"

Lt. Monty Morgan hesitated, then said with some embarrassment, "That may be slightly difficult. The families have turned to the New England Social Selection Association to make up the guest list. They are very good. Work from 18 regional Blue Books. If your name isn't there I will have to try using my influence."

"No problem. We could rent tuxedos and serve as waiters at the reception," said Fabian. "We could congratulate you and the bride between the aperitif and soup courses. Better than standing at the curb with the hoi-pol-loi tossing rice."

"I'll work with mother and see what can be done," said Monty. "If you do have to resort to that waiter bit, bill the tux rental to me."

The limousine driver shoved Monty into the Corinthian leather back seat, and the Magellan of the Army's water division drove off in a cloud of sybarite smoke.

"That's gratitude," mumbled Fabian, "and I saved him from drowning."

"You took credit for it, but we all know it was Snuffy who threw him the life ring. The only person you saved was Fabian," said Baldwin.

"It's the thought that counts and he thinks I saved him," said Fabian. "Now he won't even invite me to his wedding. Might be some good prospects for the venture capital fund I am putting together."

It was eight years later when the New York Times published a half page announcement of the wedding of Monty Morgan and Sylvia Raginfield. None of us had received an invitation, not even a rental tuxedo.

As we left the administration building Fabian was prepared to make an emotional separation speech, mostly about his new venture capital fund. "The least I can do is offer you fellows first crack at the opportunity to provide for yourself and your heirs a lifetime of prosperity and comfort. You may never have to work again." He was cut short when he spotted a civilian just outside the gate who looked like he might be a process server.

"Gotta duck for a moment. See you later." And the irresistible morale officer, Fabian Murphy, seemed to have disappeared forever. It wasn't until November 24, 1970, when I received a collect telephone call from Army reservist, Major F. Murphy.

November 24, 1970 - I knew it was Fabian Murphy when the receptionist announced that there was a long-distance collect call for me. She said the caller informed her that it was personal, which meant I would have to pay the toll. "He had a nice voice and said that if I ever visited Chicago he would be happy to show me around and make certain I didn't miss anything important."

"That is very considerate. Just be sure to wear your chastity belt," I said. "Put him on but disconnect after thirty minutes. I am paying the tab, you know."

Fabian sounded exactly as he had when we parted twenty-four years earlier at Fort Belvoir, Virginia--confident, knowledgeable, patronizing and sympathetic to those who did not see the big picture.

"Hey skipper," he said, "have you seen the book 'A Matter of Accountability?' The author identifies the PUEBLO, now in the hands of the North Koreans, as our old ship, the FS344!"

"That is an exciting bit of news," I said, "but where do you come in? Are you selling books? Did the SEC put a damper on those questionable annuities you were peddling? Monty Morgan is still trying to track you down. Wants to talk about those Texas citrus acres you sold him. Seems they are under water and full of alligators."

"Always the humorist, aren't you, Captain. I have my own well-respected securities firm. Made a lot of people rich with very little mark-up for myself, after reasonable expenses. Right now I am offering you and our old crew an opportunity to gain fame and some profit by exercising our rights as Americans and settling old scores. Our experience as crew of the ship that later became the PUEBLO is sure to get us well deserved mention in America's Marine records as patriots who took matters into their own hands."

"Are you without any ethical principles?" I said. "This is shocking. You are proposing that we capitalize on the torture and hardship suffered for more than a year by the 83 men of the PUEBLO. Their skipper was threatened with a general court-martial and they were looked upon with contempt by a Navy that had sent them into a situation of self-destruction. And you want some recognition for having gotten seasick on the non-combatant FS344? Sort of a I-knew-it-when scenario."

"Reverse your engines--you're out of control," said the former morale officer. "I don't want to get in someone else's parade. I want to recapture the PUEBLO and bring it home!"

"You must be drinking that cheap Chicago bilge water," I said. "Maybe we can get you into an Army rehab center where you can imagine you are General Custer at Little Bighorn."

"Stow the dumb wit and listen to my plan. First, we contact the old crew and fill them in on the operation. It's a sure-fire procedure they will all want to be part of."

"Fill me in," I said. "I don't want to be left out. If it is your plan it is sure to be rewarding--mostly for you--and maybe you will share some of it with me."

"It is so simple I am surprised you didn't think of it. Listen to this. The PUEBLO is moored at a pier in the North Korean port of Najin. They are always short of bucks over there so there is a charge of five dollars a head to tour this trophy of war - our ship!"

Fabian lowered his voice and in a tone of confidentiality began to outline his plan. "We are not as agile as we were when we fought to defend our country, so hand-to-hand combat is out.

This time we will use stealth and clever subterfuge to take over the ship. We will dress our crew to look like camera-toting tourists - you know, madras walking shorts and Hawaiian T-shirts. At a signal from you, our boys announce the ship is under our command, order all lines cast off and we leave the dock. Simple, isn't it? All at a cost of five dollars a person. We will get some service club - maybe Rotary - to underwrite our expenses, plane fare and other out-of-pocket costs. Simple, isn't it?"

"Why am I listening to this at thirty-five cents a minute?" I said. "How about clearing up a few details before my credit runs out. What about the standby Korean crew? Are they going to be so pleased with the five dollar tab that they help us start the engines?"

"Minor problems," said Fabian. "These guys aren't even soldiers. They are tourist guides in uniform working for their daily rice allotment, if it's a good season. We offer them the choice of being put ashore or coming with us to the U.S. where they can get a Green Card and work in the grape industry. If there is a holdout we tell them we know Marilyn Monroe and if they play their cards right they might get a date – these guys are pretty horny, you know. We may end up with more Koreans than the ship can handle. While we are taking snapshots from the bridge deck, chief engineer Ronald Cuthburt will be in the engine room getting those twin GM's humming. The rest of our guys will be taking up their old positions and we will be out to sea before the boys at the Wonsan Country Club know they have lost their number one tourist attraction."

"What happens when the Koreans send out those nasty subchasers to retrieve the PUEBLO and cut short our cruise?"

Fabian had all the answers. "As soon as we reach the 12-mile limit we start screaming over the radio to the Seventh Fleet telling them that if they want to keep their PUEBLO they better send their carrier fly-boys over here fast. When all is secure we will demand the right to sail the ship back to San Diego. May have a little problem with Monty's navigation unless he has brushed up on his dead reckoning skills. Can you just see the crowds at the pier when we come alongside? I will have joined you at the seabuoy."

"What do you mean, you will have joined us?" I said. "I know a morale officer might be a little out of place in a caper like this, but as a producer it seems appropriate that you be on the scene."

Fabian was becoming impatient. "You don't seem to understand that there is more to winning a skirmish like this than just standing on the firing line. I remain state-side to stroke the populous, beat the drum for the selfless efforts of our valiant crew, pander to the media and set up the personal appearances and book signings. I have already talked to Larry

King, Live. He wants first crack at whatever it is. Then there is the funding. Of course there will be expenses and our boys will need some remuneration for emotional stress and lost work time. Snuffy is still in service and will probably be charged with being AWOL again, but the Army will forgive him when we deliver the FS344 back to it's legal owners - the U.S. of A. Somebody back here has got to pull the right strings and keep our patriotic financial backers from losing interest."

"I am beginning to see the big picture," I said. "What about your expenses? I don't imagine you are doing all this just to get an income tax deduction. You certainly will have some stamp and stationery expenditures."

"Oh sure, there will be the ordinary overhead, but for me it will be a non-profit expression of devotion to my country. I expect that a couple of venture capital groups may want to invest in the operation, but that's their decision, not mine. So what do you say, skipper, ready to sign on?

"Fabian, I've just been signaled that my thirty minutes are up. Got to disconnect before the boss pulls the plug. Nice of you to call collect. Don't wait another twenty-four years."

"You never did have much imagination," he said. "Have you ever considered Amway? Or dog grooming?"

ABOUT THE AUTHOR

Prior to stepping forward to defend his country in 1942 William Melms had served as a cub reporter for the Detroit Free Press and later the Detroit News. After three years of service in the Army's Water Division during World War II, he returned to Michigan and joined Jacobson Stores, Inc., retiring after 35 years. Since then he has been a financial officer, hotel manager, media director and business management instructor. He retired from the Army Reserve as a Lieutenant Colonel and has appeared before service clubs and at corporate meetings as guest speaker.